T0082914

THE GREATEST PRAYERS EVER PRAYED

The Biblical Account of All the Great Prayers from Genesis to Revelation

GARY VOCHATZER

authorHOUSE®

AuthorHouse™
1663 Liberty Drive
Bloomington, IN 47403
www.authorhouse.com
Phone: 1 (800) 839-8640

© 2017 Gary Vochatzer. All rights reserved.

No part of this book may be reproduced, stored in a retrieval system, or
transmitted by any means without the written permission of the author.

Published by AuthorHouse 10/23/2017

ISBN: 978-1-5462-1067-2 (sc)
ISBN: 978-1-5462-1068-9 (e)

Print information available on the last page.

Any people depicted in stock imagery provided by Thinkstock are models,
and such images are being used for illustrative purposes only.
Certain stock imagery © Thinkstock.

This book is printed on acid-free paper.

Because of the dynamic nature of the Internet, any web addresses or links contained in
this book may have changed since publication and may no longer be valid. The views
expressed in this work are solely those of the author and do not necessarily reflect the
views of the publisher, and the publisher hereby disclaims any responsibility for them.

Holy Bible, New International Version®, NIV® Copyright ©1973, 1978, 1984,
2011 by Biblica, Inc.® Used by permission. All rights reserved worldwide.

These are the whispered, the lofty, the noble prayers of the multiple numbers of men and women chosen by God himself to utter the words written in the Holy Bible, transcribed by individuals who heard such words via the Holy Spirit. May they help you in your prayers to the "I am who I am" God of all creation:

They have been of incalculable benefit to my own journey. I would hope it is as well to you, the reader of this work. You will find in this book 124 prayers, each one God heard and each one had a benefit to someone. Could you use a prayer of these magnitudes? (And more than likely there are more than 124 prayers but these I chose for this book.)

COMMENTS

THIS BOOK TOOK HOURS TO WRITE AND YEARS TO GET IT TO BEING PUBLISHED – THAT'S THE WAY GOD WORKS! EVERYTHING IS ON HIS TIMETABLE, BE IT WE BELIEVE IT OR NOT!

THIS BOOK WAS CONCEIVED AND WRITTEN WITH THE MIND OF GOD BEHIND IT 100 %, SO KNOWING THAT, I CANNOT TAKE AN OUNCE OF CREDIT FOR SUCH AS YOU ARE TO READ!

THANKS TO CECILE KAISER AND THE LOCAL TYPIST FOR ALL THEIR HELP.

YOU CAN REACH ME IF ANY QUESTIONS, VIA MY WEBSITES:
WWW.WHISPEREDTO.COM
WWW.THEONESTOPINSURANCESHOP.COM
EMAIL: garyjv3940@yahoo.com

MY OTHER BOOKS PUBLISHED TO DATE:

WHISPERED TO, VOL. 1	(POETRY)
WHISPERED TO, VOL. 2	(POETRY)
A PRAYER JOURNAL	(BOOK)
JOB	(BOOK)
SECOND CHANCE	(BOOK)
ESTHER	(BOOK)

THANK YOU

OLD TESTAMENT PRAYERS AND WHY THEY WERE PRAYED

TABLE OF CONTENTS OLD TESTAMENT

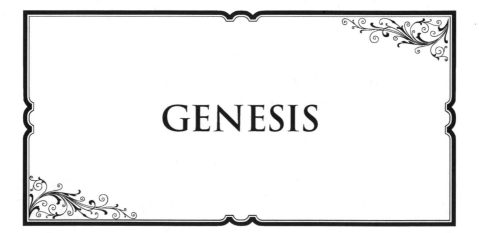

GENESIS

GENESIS 18:22-33

God remained with Abraham while the other two angelic angels moved on to Sodom and Gomorrah. Abraham went toward God to ask in this prayer. Will you kill the good with the evil in this village? Let us suppose I could find fifty godly individuals. Would you still destroy it and kill the fifty as well the multitude of evil? Surely that can't be correct, if so both evil and good are treated in the same manner. You, being God I am confident would not do such knowing well you're the judge of all humanity.

What if forty-five were found?
What if forty were found?
What if thirty were found?
What if twenty were found?
What if ten were found?

In all God said He would not destroy even if found only ten godly.

PURPOSE OF PRAYER

Abraham's relatives lived in this city and were, by pleading, hoping he could get God to spare their lives!

GENESIS 20:17-18

Abraham prayed to God, asking Him to cure the king and queen and all the women of their household so that those able, could bear children, for it was God alone who struck these women to cause barrenness in order to punish Abimelech for trying to steal Abraham's wife to be his own.

PURPOSE OF PRAYER

As Abraham was traveling to the place God was leading, he had stopped in a location where a king resided, and being in fear of this king, he told all that Sarah, his wife, was his sister. Sure enough, the king, seeing Sarah's beauty, took her to be his wife. But God intervened and told the king in a dream he best not sleep with Sarah and to return her to her husband, Abraham.... which he promptly did.

GENESIS 24:12-14

Oh, Lord of my master, Abraham. Please be kind to him in all things, and help me accomplish the task he has sent me forth to do on this journey I am on – and now I ask You, as I am here next to this spring and the women are coming to draw water – when I say to the one you lead me to, "May I have a drink of that cool fresh water," she will in turn say "Yes," and "as well, I will water your camels." Then Lord, let her be the one you say is to be Isaac's new wife – by this I will know my journey is a success.

PURPOSE OF PRAYER

Abraham, being very elderly, told his servant that Isaac, his son, is not allowed to marry a woman outside the race of Judaism, or a non-Israelite, and instructed him to travel to a distant relative and find a wife for Isaac there, and to cement it on the servant, an angel from God would go before him and choose the right wife for Isaac.

GENESIS 24:15-27

Oh, Lord, my Master's God, please I plead with you to show your kindness and mercy to Abraham in order I may, at your timing, accomplish the goal I was sent to do. Notice I am here next to this spring of water and the ladies of the village are moving toward this spring to draw up water.

My request, Lord, is for you to have the one I was chosen to speak to ask her for a drink of water. She will answer "Yes plus I will get water for your camels as well." Let her be Isaac's future bride.

PURPOSE OF PRAYER

Abraham's servants well knew the faith he had in the God he worshipped so they had faith in this same God!

GENESIS 28:20-22

If the Lord God will protect me... help me... on this journey I am on, and provide food and clothing and as well, will return me safely to my father, Isaac, then I as well, will choose the God Abraham worshiped and my father worships to be my God.

PURPOSE OF PRAYER

Jacob had stopped for a night's rest. He had put his camels down and laid his head on a rock to go to sleep. He dreamed he saw a staircase going to and from earth and heaven and angels going back and forth – and at its top, God stood and told Jacob the land he slept on was his and all his future descendants, and they would be as the stars in the skies, and as well, told Jacob He would be his protector from that moment forward. Jacob awoke and prayed this prayer.

GENESIS 32:9-12

Oh, the God of Abraham and my father, Isaac, Your goodness to me is far greater than a mere man could expect. You told me to return home and I would be safe. I have listened and again, I say, I am not worthy of an ounce of Your goodness, for when I left my home, my only possession was a walking stick, and now, because of You – two armies are at my command. But my prayer, Lord, is this... don't allow my brother, Esau, to destroy not only me, but my family as well. Yet, Lord, recall Your promise to me that my descendants will be as the sand pebbles that lay on the seashores.

PURPOSE OF PRAYER

Jacob had stolen Esau's birthright and blessing and then ran away from his homeland as his mother Rebekah told him to do. He stayed away for eons, marrying and having children and growing an estate. Yet, when God told him to return to his homeland, fear gripped him of his brother Esau's revenge.

GENESIS 32:22-32

As Jacob returned to his camp and was alone a man began to wrestle with Jacob and it lasted till sunrise and when this man saw he was unable to win the struggle he struck Jacob's hip and knocked it out of joint. At that the man said, "It's sunrise, let me go."

But Jacob prayed out "Not until you bless me."

Then the man asked Jacob what his name was. Jacob said, "Jacob." Then the man said no more.

"Your new name is Israel for you have power with the God of Israel and prevail you will."

Jacob asked the man's name and no answer came forward. Jacob then named this prayer incident Peniel for it means one has seen the face of God and lived to tell of it.

PURPOSE OF PRAYER

Jacob wanted to be blessed as his father Isaac was blessed so here he saw an opportunity to do such and did.

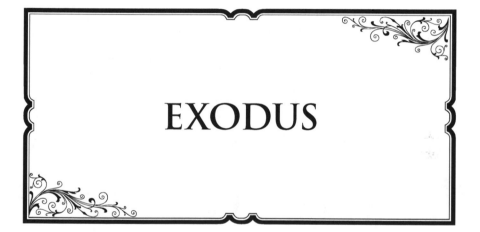

EXODUS

EXODUS 2:23-25

Years later the Pharaoh who was kind to the Jews died and the new Pharaoh had a different view on the Jewish community and made it impossible to simply bear life and the cries of the Jews were heard by God and hearing them He recalled His promise to Abraham, Jacob, Isaac which was to bring them back to the land of Canaan. He saw their plight, heard their moans and said it's time for their rescue.

PURPOSE OF PRAYER

God hears those who cry out to Him, especially His own, chosen by His family.

EXODUS 32:11-14

Lord, why are You so angry, so heated against Your own family whom You saved from the land of Egypt and did it with such miraculous miracles none can match.

Do you really want the world to say their god fooled them bringing them out to this waste land only to slay each one of them?

I plead with you to turn from such anger, don't allow this wrath fall to down upon Your own elect, recall Your promise to our forefathers that You would multiply the Jews as the stars in the heavens or the sand on the ocean shores. Don't allow, Lord, this promise by You to be broken by You!

PURPOSE OF PRAYER

Moses begged God to not do what He was about to do and God listened to this human being and put away His anger.

EXODUS 33:12-13

Lord, You have told me to take these people of yours to the Promised Land, yet You have not told me who You are sending with me. You have said You're my friend, and that I have found favor with You, so hearing that from You, would You please guide me on the road You have chosen for me to travel on.... that way, I can understand You and walk acceptable to You, and Lord, let's not forget this nation is your people.

PURPOSE OF PRAYER

Moses spoke this prayer inside the sacred tent God had instructed to build, and he was again pleading with God to give him assurance all he was doing – and the place they were – and the direction in which they were going was all in alignment with God's leading.

EXODUS 34:9

Oh, Lord, if it is true that I have found favor with You, then please, I plead, go with us – stay next to us on this road to the Promised Land, and yes, I agree this is a stubborn and unruly nation of people – yet, pardon our faults / our sins / our inequities and simply accept us as Your own choosing.

PURPOSE OF PRAYER

Moses prayed this as God spoke to him as if one man talking to another, yet Moses feeling extremely inadequate of the job ahead issued this prayer after God spoke to him.

NUMBERS

NUMBERS 11:11-15

Oh, Lord, I have to ask of You... why did You choose me for such an awesome task. These are not my children, they are Yours. You are their Father, not me. Yet You have chosen me for this audacious task of nursing these babies until we arrive at the Promised Land which You had promised to their forefathers, but Lord, how am I to feed them as I am only one individual and cannot carry this huge burden alone, as the weight is too great to carry – if You won't remove these obstacles, then I suggest You kill me now, as it would be far better than the responsibility at hand – either take over or get me out of here.

PURPOSE OF PRAYER

Moses was hearing the crying / the moaning / the weeping / the yelling at God for bringing them here in a desert with not knowing to go South / East / West / North / and bottom line is that put Moses in a depression so bad he begged to die.

NUMBERS 12:13

Lord – heal Miriam of this disease You laid on her... Please, I beg of You – heal her Lord.

PURPOSE OF PRAYER

Aaron and Miriam were chastising Moses simply because his wife was a non-Hebrew and God heard it all. He called all three to the Tabernacle and gave both Aaron and Miriam a tongue-lashing for their criticism. Soon after Miriam was stuck with leprosy and became as white as snow.

NUMBERS 14:13-19

Okay, Lord, yet I ask, what will Egypt say of this? They saw how You rescued this family of yours and they have spread the word of Your power like seed thrown on the ground. They have told of how You chose Israel as Your own and how You speak face to face with me, Your servant, and as well, how You lead us 24/7 – yet if You destroy them all, the same word will go out saying Your power wasn't strong enough to care for their needs / wasn't strong enough to get them to the land You had promised them – so again, I plead – show Your patience / show Your forgiveness / show Your love / and yes, sin does not go unpunished – be it the individual or the sons that follow – yet, I ask now / forgive this unruly people because of Your love for them, just as You have since the beginning of Your choosing them to be your family.

PURPOSE OF PRAYER

God was disgusted with all the whining / despair / and especially, unbelief after seeing all the miracles He had performed right before their eyes – so He tells Moses, He is going to kill them all and save Moses only.

NUMBERS 16:22

Aaron and Moses fell face down on the ground itself and prayed out, "Oh, Lord of all humankind must You be angry at all for one man's sins?"

PURPOSE OF PRAYER

Three individuals had sinned against God and God was going to destroy the whole lot, but because Aaron and Moses prayed this prayer only these three and all their families and earthly treasures were destroyed in an instant of time.

DEUTERONOMY

DEUTERONOMY 9:26-29

Oh Lord, I ask again... do not destroy this nation as they are Yours, saved from the strong arm of Egypt by Your awesome power. Pay no attention to their crying and whining / stubbornness or rebellion, but instead, recall Your promises to Abraham / Isaac / Jacob – overlook their wickedness and sin – but if You kill them, all the world will simply say, "God was not able, which was proven by His marching them out into the wilds and killing them there." These are Your own. Save them from Your destruction.

PURPOSE OF PRAYER

God is angry / disgusted / at such as He chose to be His own to the point He feels it's best to wipe them out and start over.

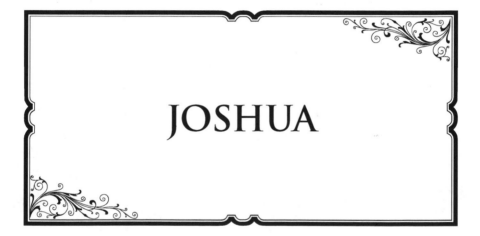

JOSHUA

JOSHUA 7:7-9

Why, Lord, would You bring us across the Jordan River on dry land if You close your eyes to the power of the Amorites overtaking us by slaughter? Why did we cross over when contentment was already in the camp? Why did we cross over when all was well where we were? The Israeli Army has fled this power and when the surrounding nations hear of our weakness, they will attack us as ants attack a piece of meat, and at that, what will the world say of your power in protecting us?

PURPOSE OF PRAYER

Joshua was frustrated / in fear / felt lonely / abandoned / hopeless / helpless / and so went to God with all his anxieties and laid them on Him to deal with.

JOSHUA 10:12

"Oh, Lord, allow the sun to stand still over Gibeon and allow the moon to as well, stand still over the valley of Aijalon."

PURPOSE OF PRAYER

Joshua was in a winning mind set as he was well aware it was not he nor the Israeli military that had power, but it was the power of God battling the enemy and winning each war waged – and God answered Joshua by allowing the sun to stay in the sky at its same position 24 hours while he and his army fought the battle of God in human form.

JUDGES

JUDGES 15:18

You have blessed Israel with an awesome deliverance from its enemies today and used me to see it through. Must I now, Lord, die of thirst and fall to the very enemy you defeated?

PURPOSE OF PRAYER

Samson had just killed one thousand Philistine military with the jawbone of a donkey. In the end, as he looked over the field of the dead, he became deathly thirsty and prayed to God about it, and God answered him at his prayer's end.

JUDGES 16:28

Oh, Lord Jehovah, will You please remember me just one more time. Put within me the strength once again, so that You may have the glory in paying back these Philistines for the tearing out of just one of my eyes.

PURPOSE OF PRAYER

Because of Samson's letting down his guard, he allowed Delilah to deceive him and he was captured by his arch enemy. They tortured him beyond description. Then, at a grand party, they put him on display to show their power, but God has an idea – He allowed Samson the strength to push the pillars apart that held up the entire coliseum, killing all within.

1ST SAMUEL

1ˢᵀ SAMUEL 2:1-10

Oh, how I praise the Lord. How He has blessed me – And now my enemies can be answered, for God has solved my dilemma... and how I magnify His name for no one is as holy as the Lord I serve. There are no other gods, nor is there a Rock as that of the Lord we worship, yet we act as if we were as He is... making us fools among ourselves. The Lord's eyes roam earth as an eagle soars above the skies seeing all that goes on – and, yes, God judges fairly, those who were strong are now weak – those who were weak are now strong – those who had it made are now starving – those who were starving are now fed – the barren woman was blessed with seven children, she will have no more – The Lord kills, yet the same Lord gives life. The Lord makes the rich and the poor. The Lord puts one down and lifts another up. He picks up the poor as ashes and then treats them as princes. He seats them in chairs of honor. All the earth belongs to God, for it is He who set all in its order – It is He who will protect His Godly ones – yet, the wicked shall only see darkness and only hear silence – not one person can succeed by strength alone for those who take up battle with God shall surely be broken – His thunder roars from heaven – He judges the earth and its inhabitants – He puts power into the king of His choice and heaps great glory on His anointed one.

PURPOSE OF PRAYER

Hannah was Elkanah's wife, yet she was barren during their marriage, but his other wife was able to produce children. One night, she went to the church and prayed a prayer which God heard. In it, she vowed if she could have a child she would return the child to Him to be of service in the church. Surely, soon after she bore a son and named him Samuel, and sure enough, as a small child, Hannah gave him to Eli, the priest, at that time.

2ND SAMUEL

2ND SAMUEL 7:18-29

Oh, Lord, what have I done and who am I to be so blessed by You – You have showered down upon me blessings beyond my imagination – and to add to this, you tell me You're giving me an eternal dynasty. Such blessings are far above human comprehension – what can I say? What words can thank you for your generosity – You of all, know who I am and yet you bless me anyway – Yet you're not a promise breaker and because of that commitment you're keeping it while humanity would toss it aside. How great Thou art – who has heard of such a God as You? And yes, Lord, there are no other gods but You – who else can boast of what You have done for Israel, this nation You have taken under Your wing as an eagle does its young. It was You and You alone that has rescued Israel from its enemies since the day You chose to take them as Your own –

You, Lord, destroyed Egypt and all its manmade gods to bring glory to Your name and save this people You call your own – You have decided Israel is Yours and Israel has chosen You to be their God – so now, Lord, keep Your promise concerning me and my family, and may for all time, may You be honored by Israel and this dynasty You have blessed me with as well, last forever – You have, Lord, whispered to me, saying that I am the first in a long history, yet to unfold that will lead this nation of Yours – and yes, Lord, this is what has put this boldness in me to pray a prayer as I have here at this time. I accept the challenge – You are the God of all there is, and all You say is truth, so thank You for all the good You're going to do for me – do as You committed to do – bless me and my family forever – and may our family continue forever in time – thank you, Lord.

PURPOSE OF PRAYER

God had spoken to Nathan, the prophet, and told him what He would do with David, His chosen servant, and when Nathan told David what God had said, David prayed this prayer.

1ST KINGS

1st KINGS 3:6-9

Oh, Lord of all – How wonderful You were to my father, David, because he made a choice to be honest in all things, and truthful in all things, and faithful to You by obeying You and now Your blessings continue as You are doing through the son You gave King David – You have made me king, Lord, passed onto me from my father – yet, Lord, I am as a child, not knowing which direction to take, and among a nation with so many lives it would be an impossibility to count – so Lord, I ask of You, give my mind an understanding so I can govern this nation of Yours to what is right and run from what is wrong – for I ask, who can accept such an enormous responsibility without Your involvement.

PURPOSE OF PRAYER

God appeared to Solomon in a dream and said to him, "Ask anything you wish and it will be granted."

1ST KINGS 8:12-13

The Lord God said He would live in the thickness of dark, yet Lord, I have built for You a home here on earth, a place for You to live forever in time.

PURPOSE OF PRAYER

Solomon called a gathering of all the leaders of Israel to pray two prayers – this is his first.

1ST KINGS 8:22-53

Oh, Lord God over Israel, there is no other God as You in heaven and on earth. You are a loving and kind God, and a God who keeps a promise if those You commit to do their utmost in keeping Your will tied to their hearts – today Lord, You have fulfilled your commitment to my father, David, who was a servant of Yours, chosen by You.

Now Lord, I ask You to make Your commitment complete by allowing one of my father's descendants to forever be a king so long as they seek Your will in every way. Fulfill this promise, Lord, I ask of You – and Lord, may it be a possibility that You could truly live here on earth for the skies and all of the heavens cannot contain who You are much less this temple I have built just for Your presence.

Yes, Lord, all my requests have caught Your attention, and You likewise, answered in an awesome way – watch over this temple, Your home on earth – don't take Your eyes off it for a moment's time – and Lord, as well, when I come to face this temple night or day, I ask You to hear my pleas and answer accordingly. Listen to the request of Your people as they face this home of Yours, and as You listen to each one, I ask You, forgive those who ask of You.

If a man stands facing this temple, and has been accused of a wrong, and he swears he is innocent of such, then hear in heaven and You judge according to Your ways, and when sin enters into the people's hearts, and their enemies overtake them, yet they again confess their wrongdoing, bring them back to this land which You gave to their fathers.

And Lord, when the skies close up as a barren womb, and the rain hides like a deer in the forest, all because of the nation's sin, then God, hear their confession of their wrongdoing, and after You have dealt with their sin, help them back to the road to recovery in a relationship with You, and then open the skies as a dam bursting to allow the water to again soak the land, You have so freely given to this people – and Lord, if the land can bear no food from it because of disease or pestilence or Israel's enemies overtake them – or if an epidemic or plague over-shadows them – whatever, Lord, the situation may be, and the people wake to their sin, and pray as they look upon this temple – my plea is You hear their cries – their confession – and forgive them Lord knowing as You do each and every heart who confesses – by them doing this, they will find confidence in honoring You Lord as You allow them to live on this precious land – and Lord, as the world hears of all You have done for Israel, and they come to see for themselves, and they as well, stand before this temple and pray – I beg You as well, forgive their sins whatever they may be – and this hearing will also put on notice to the world that You should be as feared and honored as Israel does, and they as well will know this is Your home – Your temple – also Lord, help those who go into battle, that if they look toward Jerusalem and this temple, You, as well, will help them in their fight and defend the Holy Land.

And Lord, when the people sin (and they will), and You find anger with them so that You allow their enemies to drag them to another land and then they awaken to the fact they have sinned against You and cry out, "Oh, Lord, we have sinned / we were in error," and they, with honest hearts, pray looking toward this city and this temple, You will, in heaven, hear their cry – hear their prayer – hear their confession – and will come to their defense. Oh, Lord, forgive their evilness – and, as well, make their enemies kind and merciful to them – these Your people – Your family – Your inheritance. You saved them from Egypt, now save them again, Lord. May You always hear their voices – their weeping, for it was Moses You told that this people would be Yours forever in time, regardless of how many nations arise on this earth.

PURPOSE OF PRAYER

This was his second prayer in front of all those of importance in the nation of Israel.

He stood before the altar of God, with his hands spread out towards heaven and spoke.

1ˢᵀ KINGS 17:20

Oh, Lord, my God, I beg of You, please don't allow this child to die, but instead Lord, return His spirit within Him – Please.

PURPOSE OF PRAYER

The prophet, Elijah, had stopped to stay at a widow and her son's home. While there, the son became sick and died – and the woman screamed at Elijah, blaming him for such a tragedy.

1ˢᵀ KINGS 18:36-37

Oh, Lord, the God of Abraham, Isaac and Jacob – called Israel – prove this day, You are who You are – the true God of this nation, Israel. I am but a servant of Yours, so my plea, Lord, is to show proof that all that is happening here is as You commanded me. Answer, Lord, in a way these people will know You are God, and that You have brought them back to You.

PURPOSE OF PRAYER

Elijah, the prophet, had been harassed and threatened by one of the surrounding area kings and his Mrs. – as they worshiped a god known as Baal. So a test between their god and the God Elijah worshiped and followed was set on Mount Carmel to find out which God was alive and active or dead and buried.

1ˢᵀ KINGS 19:4

Oh, Lord, I have had it – take my life today – I have to die someday, so let's agree today is the day.

PURPOSE OF PRAYER

Elijah ran from the fear he may be killed by the king and his Mrs. He had come to a spot out in the wilderness – tired – hungry – worn out – he laid down.

2ND KINGS

2ND KINGS 6:17

Oh, Lord, open his eyes and let him see.

2ND KINGS 6:19

Oh, Lord, make them all blind.

2ND KINGS 6:20

Oh, Lord, allow their eyes to be open and let them see.

PURPOSE OF PRAYERS

The king of Syria was adamant in finding and killing Elisha because he, through God, was able to tell the Israelites what the enemy's plans were.

One night, the king sent an army to capture Elisha, and at daybreak, when the prophet's servant open the door to see what kind of day it was, he was awestruck in fear of the multitude of Syrian military – but Elisha arose and told him, "Don't be afraid, for God's military is much greater"... and it was. He then, because of their blindness, had them all travel to Samaria, the very capital of Israel.

2ND KINGS 19:15-19

Oh, Lord, the God of Israel, way above the angels, sitting upon Your throne. You and You alone are the God of all creation... the kingdoms that reside on earth – You allowed... the heavens above, and this earth You created. So, Lord, I plea to You, bend so low You can see and hear the defiant tongue of this Assyrian king who riles against Your very name.

Yes, he has destroyed nation after nation, and has burned up manmade gods people worship... yet we know they were not gods, but simple human puny ideas of a god they created. But now, Lord, our plea to You is to save us from such an awesome power as these Assyrian kings have demonstrated.... By Your doing this, the world will assuredly know You are the only true God to be worshiped.

PURPOSE OF PRAYER

King Hezekiah had been told an army greater than known before was about to destroy Israel, yet God told Isaiah, the prophet, to tell King Hezekiah not to worry, it was all in God's hands, and He would resolve it in His way.

2ND KINGS 20:2-3

King Hezekiah put his face towards the wall and prayed, "Oh God, please recall how I have run after You, being obedient to Your every word and to work at pleasing You in all I do on this journey I am on."

After this prayer he fell to his knees and cried in deep remorse.

PURPOSE OF PRAYER

Isaiah, the Prophet had told him to get his affairs in order that it was time to meet those who had died previously.

1ST CHRONICLES

1ST CHRONICLES 4:10

Oh, Lord, Your deciding to bless me is too wonderful to put in mere words, and to help me in my work is an added blessing. My one request, Lord, is to help me in all I do, and to keep evil and disaster away from my journey.

PURPOSE OF PRAYER

Jabez was a descendent in the tribe of Judah. He had a different look to him, and stood out among his brothers. His mother named him Jabez because he was a difficult child to deliver at his birth, as the name, Jabez, means in Hebrew, "Distress."

1ST CHRONICLES 17:16-27

Oh Lord, who am I to be blessed as You have done with me? What is my family that You should look so graciously upon them? Yet, Lord, none of what's been requested thus far can remotely compare to the promises You have made for the future. You're telling me of future generations where my children will be honored as I am this day. Oh, Lord, You talk as if I were someone special, yet You know I am but a puff of air / a speck of sand / nothing but a simple human being... yet for Your reasons, You have chosen me to be honored. I am in awe. Is it, Lord, just because as simple as I can put it... You want to be kind to me and because You have a heart of love.... incomparable to the human heart. You, Lord, are alone in who You are for who can even touch Your awesomeness? You are the only God the earth and heavens revere. No other god as You is known by humankind. And, Lord, what nation can boast of a god as You, taking on Israel as Your own. You saved it from Egypt and have in Your own way, made it special to You. These people are Your people, and Your name, Lord, has been given great honor as You have driven out the enemies that would have destroyed Israel... had You allowed. You declared it to be the way it is and, therefore, Israel is Yours and You are what makes Israel... So, Lord, I accept this awesome promise You have made to me, and to my future children... and may this promise always bring great honor to Your name... and, Lord, may You always keep what You say You're going to do for this people You have chosen amongst the multitudes on earth. May Israel always proclaim, "The Lord of heaven cares for Israel," and may my future children as well, always lead this nation of Yours... You have put in to me, Lord, the courage to pray a prayer as this, so, I thank You. Thank You for Your promises and may they last forever... for when You, Lord, grant a blessing, it is an eternal blessing.

PURPOSE OF PRAYER

God spoke with Nathan, the prophet, and told him to tell David to forget about building Him a home on earth, but to remind Him of who he is and what he has, for it all came from the hand of God, just because that's the way God intended it to be.

1ST CHRONICLES 21:17

David said to God, "It is I who sinned by ordering this census. What has your family done in this matter. Destroy me and all my family but don't charge this sin against the innocent!"

PURPOSE OF PRAYER

All David's leaders and prophets told him not to build up his pride by ordering a census of the Israel nation. He took not their advice and God was set to destroy Israel.

1ˢᵀ CHRONICLES 29:10-19

Oh, the Lord, the Father of Israel... Praise Your holy name, Lord, forever and ever... You're the Power / You're the Glory / You're the Victor / You're the Majesty... all is Yours, Lord, be it in the heavens or on this earth... it's all Yours... Yes, this kingdom You created, is Yours and we love You for being in total control of all that there is... all the riches / all the honor is handed out by You and You alone. You rule this creation of Yours, and Your hand is always in control, be they power or might. It is Your choice, whom You are to make rich and powerful... and for that, Lord, we praise and honor You.

Yet, Lord, who are we... who am I, that we should even be given the privilege to give anything to You, for You, Lord, have given to us all that we have, so we only give back what You have given us. Yes, Lord, it is a fact that we are here for but a moment in time... yes, strangers on a land You gave to our fathers, and our days, as our father's days, are but a shadow, soon gone... not even a trace to be found.

This material, Lord, gathered up to build You a temple, all came from You... it is all Yours and Your doing. And yes, Lord, I am well aware You have a testing rule that tells You if a man is good or evil... for I am well aware it's the goodness in man that brings You great joy to see such, and know, Lord, all I have done thus far has had good intention and solid motives to honor You. And You, Lord, have seen your people bring gifts willingly and joyfully, just as I have. Oh, Lord, I plead with You... You the God of Abraham / Isaac/ Israel, make this people of Yours always want to obey You in all things, and put within them a love for You that never fails. And, Lord, put into my son, Solomon, a heart that clings to Yours so that he chases after doing what's right in even the smallest detail, and last, Lord, put within me the eagerness to complete this temple as all is here ready to do so.

PURPOSE OF PRAYER

David, standing before an awesome crowd of his own people, praises God for all his blessings that have been handed down by his heavenly Father.

2ND CHRONICLES

2ND CHRONICLES 1:8-10

Oh, God, You have been too kind to me, as You were with my father, David. In addition, You have added this kingdom... what more could one ask for. You have fulfilled all Your promises to my father, and now You have declared me king over a nation with as many a people as the dust that blows in the wind. Now, Lord, I ask You to favor me with wisdom and knowledge to rule Your people as You want me to... for who is able, Lord, to govern by themselves, such a nation as You call Your own.

PURPOSE OF PRAYER

This is the prayer Solomon prayed in front of all those of importance in Israel. This prayer was made in 1st Kings 3:6-9.

2ND CHRONICLES 6:1-2

The Lord spoke saying He would live in the thick of darkness, yet I have built a temple for You and You alone, God. May You live here forever, Lord.

PURPOSE OF PRAYER

Solomon spoke this to God as he dedicated the temple he built for God.

2ND CHRONICLES 6:14-42

Oh, Lord, the God over Israel, as You're like no other god in all of heaven and earth. You never break a promise to those who pray after obeying You and are living to do Your will. It is evident, You have kept Your promise to my father, David, and I ask You to continue that promise by always having a descendant rule over Israel, if they follow Your laws to the letter... as I have put my best effort in doing so.

Please fulfill the promise... but it is asked, "Will God truly live on earth with His creation for all the heavens and earth as well cannot contain Your presence?" So how can this temple I have built for You do so? Oh, Lord, how I plead, You will hear my prayers... listen as I seek Your attention... look down with favor upon this temple, never taking Your eyes from it. This place, Your name sits upon, so may You always hear me and answer me as I face this temple of Yours and pray to You. Listen, Lord, to my prayers, and those of Your people, as they pray looking to this temple of Yours, and as You hear us, Lord, forgive us please.

When one is caught in a crime and confesses before this temple they are innocent, then You judge and punish if they lie, otherwise, You declare them innocent, Lord.

If Your people are beaten in a war because they have sinned against You, yet if they turn to You and admit they are Yours and pray towards Your temple, then please, hear them from Your heavenly place and forgive their errors and allow them to regain this land You gave to their fathers.

And, Lord, when You shut the door to the rains because of Your people's sins, and then they come to their senses and pray toward this temple of Yours, pleading for Your forgiveness for their sins.... forgive them, please. Then teach them what is right from wrong, and on Your timetable, send rain to this land You have said is their property.

And, if a famine steps in... or a plague stops by... or a disease visits...

or a bug marches in... or if their enemy runs into their cities... or whatever besets upon Your people, then listen, Lord, to their individual prayers and the public prayers, as well. Hear all of it in heaven, and Lord, forgive and pass judgment or blessing on each as deserved... as You know, Lord, the hearts of each creation You alone created. They will reverence You, Lord... and, yes, will take the path You lead them on. And, even when foreigners hear of Your awesome power and travel great distances to see it for themselves, and they, as well, pray toward this temple, hear them also, Lord, and answer their prayers, as You so lovingly do ours, then they will also acknowledge this temple built for You is Yours and Yours alone.

And, Lord, when You send Your people out to battle the enemies, and they pray for success, then I ask You to grant it to them. And, if they sin against You, as all humankind does, and Your anger flares up against them, and You allow their enemies to defeat them and haul off many to other lands.... yet, while there, and they pray looking towards this temple, pleading for Your forgiveness, then hear from heaven, and do forgive them, Lord. Put Your ear to this temple so that when prayers are spoken to You, You're hearing them... So enter, Lord, Your home, where the Ark of the Covenant is... allow Your priest to be clothed in salvation and let Your people praise You for Your kindness towards them... don't turn from me, Lord... Don't walk away... Don't ignore me, Lord... Don't turn Your face from me, Your chosen one... Recall, Lord, Your kindness and love toward my father, David.

PURPOSE OF PRAYER

Solomon prayed this prayer in 1st Kings 8:22-52, and the writer of 1st and 2nd Chronicles, Ezra, is simply going over the history of the nation Israel.

2ND CHRONICLES 14:11

Oh Lord, You're our only hope for who else but You can help us. We are powerless against such a massive military. Help us, God, for it is You alone we put our trust in to rescue us from such as we face, yet in Your holy name, we go after this huge horde of our enemy. Don't allow, Lord, mere men to defeat You, please.

PURPOSE OF PRAYER

Asa was the king over Judah and was a king who looked toward God's blessing, and because of that, God gave Judah peace. A military of 300,000 men obeyed his command and another 280,000 Benjaminites as well obeyed him, yet the kings of Ethiopia, with 1,000,000 brave souls, were about to attack the nation of Israel – knowing they were outnumbered 2 to 1, Asa prayed this prayer.

2ND CHRONICLES 20:6-12

Oh Lord, the God of all our forefathers. The one and only God who resides over heaven... the Ruler over all humanity... You are a most powerful God... for who has the strength to stand against You. Wasn't it You, Lord who drove out all those who resided in this land You gave to Israel. And wasn't it You, Lord, who gave all this and to Abraham on a forever basis. It is Your people, Lord who reside here now... Your people built this temple... dedicated to You, Lord, with the faith that especially in dire times as these, we could stand here facing Your home, crying out to save us, Lord. When tragedies such as war / disease / famine come, You are here to deliver us from such calamities... so hear us now, Lord, please. You see what's building up against us... the militaries of Ammon / Moab / Mount Seir.

You, at the time we marched out of Egypt toward this land, told our ancestors – led by Moses – to not invade / attack these nations and they bypassed them in their march to the Promised land. Now our reward comes from obeying and leaving them alone, for they march to put us off this land You promised to our fathers. Stop them, Lord. Put a halt to their goal. We are but ants against such a vast military, so we look to You to save us, for who but You can we count on?

PURPOSE OF PRAYER

Jehoshaphat was king over Judah and during his time, three nations declared war on its kingdom of God. He sought God's help and even pronounced a fasting to prove the people were depending on God for security. He prayed this prayer pleading to God.

EZRA

EZRA 9:5-15

My God, my God, I am ashamed / embarrassed / and blush to even look up to You. The sin of all of us is head deep, if not higher, and our guilt in the same degree. Yes, Lord, I agree with You... we are a nation with a history of sin, and because of the path we chose, kings and priests have been killed by heathen nations / captured / robbed / disgraced / has been our trial... just as it is this day... yet you saw in us which we are blinded to a moment in time where peace abides, for You permitted a small minority of us to find our way back to Jerusalem from those who held us captive. A tiny fraction of joy amongst our enslavement... for You know, Lord, we were slaves, but for Your own reasons, You decided to not abandon us to that dire state of being, but instead, you stepped in on our behalf and put within the minds of the kings of Persia to be kind to us, and not only that gift, but they are assisting us in the rebuilding of this great temple of Yours, and in addition to that, they are helping rebuild the walled city in Judah.

Yet, Lord, what can be said after Your boundless love to us continues even as we break Your laws and turn our backs to obeying You. Yes, the prophets of past spoke about those living on the land You gave us being defiled by the practices of evilness. North to South and East to West sin abounded. You said to us, "Do not allow your daughters to marry the sons of this corrupted people nor allow your sons to marry their daughters nor to help in any way whatsoever." And You said if we held to this law, You would prosper us beyond our imagination and this prosperity would pass onto each generation.

Yet, now Lord, even as we sit in exile because sin envelopes us and punishment lays in our beds and even though You allowed a few of us to return home, we have failed You as usual, and did what You said not to do – intermarry with those you said not to marry. Surely, Your anger will desolate us again, and this time, not even a remnant will remain.

You are a fair and just God... what may I ask or hope for as we abound in sin against the laws you set before us. We are most certainly evil before You.

PURPOSE OF PRAYER

Ezra had been given the right, by his captors, to go back to Jerusalem to rebuild the city and inhabit it once again. And while there, he was told of the marriages of Jewish people, including priests and Levite men, to non-Jewish woman... and so Ezra saw nothing but pollution amongst those who he thought were obeying God, so he prayed this prayer.

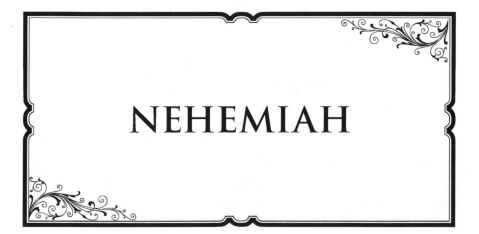

NEHEMIAH

NEHEMIAH 1:5-11

Oh Lord, You are an awesome God who never, ever breaks a promise, and is loving and kind to those who love You and are obedient to You. Oh God, hear my prayer. Put Your ear to my heart as it speaks, Lord... look down from heaven and see me as I pray day and night for this family that is Yours, the people of Israel... and, I agree with Your saying that we have sinned against You, Lord, a horrible sin.

The sin is we have neglected the Ten Commandments You gave to Moses for us to abide by. You told Moses, "If you sin you will be scattered as mosquitoes in the wind... yet, if you decide to return to my laws and obey, no matter how far you are from your homeland, I will clear a path for your return home, for it is in Jerusalem I have made a home for Myself."

Yes, Lord, we are but servants, the people You saved by Your awesome power... so please, Lord, hear me. Oh, hear us, Lord, as we pray, and especially to those who find it vital to obey Your every word.

Oh Lord, help me at this moment... at this place... and Lord, be with my tongue / my mind / my speech as I prepare to address the king to plead with him for a favor, and as well as Lord, put within him a kind heart to be gentle with me.

PURPOSE OF PRAYER

Nehemiah prayed this because He was told that the Jerusalem walls still lay in desolation so he wanted God's help asking the king to let him go to this rubble.

NEHEMIAH 4:4-5

Oh Lord, hear us as we are being scorned / mocked / laughed at in the rebuilding of Your wall here in Your city. May You, Lord, allow their ridicule to harm them as they attempt to dissuade us from such a duty. May You send them off as captured goats, and do not, Lord, fail to recall their ignorance for just as they taunt us, they as well, do it to You when they do it to us.

PURPOSE OF PRAYER

Nehemiah prayed this as progress was slow in the rebuilding of the wall in Jerusalem, and they were taunted at such a work.

NEHEMIAH 6:14

Oh Lord, my God, please do not forget the evil of these rascals Tobiah / Sanballat and Noadiah, the prophetess and all the other prophets who have tried in vain to discourage me.

PURPOSE OF PRAYER

Nehemiah was diligent at the rebuilding of the walls of Jerusalem, but everywhere he turned, obstacles arose... in particular... those mentioned in his prayer as they had plans to kill him.

NEHEMIAH 9:6-38

Oh Lord, You are the only God in all creation... as it is You who created all that there is / the skies / the heavens / the earth / the seas / and all that lives within them. You alone preserve all You have created and the heavenly angels worship You in adoration.

It was You, Lord, who chose Abram and caused him to go from Ur of the Chaldeans to his next destination and You, Lord, changed his name to Abraham... and when You read his heart and knew he could be faithful, You made an eternal contract with him ... forever giving him and his future descendants all the lands of the Canaanites / Hittites / Amorites / Perizzites / Jebusites and the Girgashites... and You never break a commitment.

It was You, Lord, who saw the heartache of our ancestors in Egypt as You heard their cries as they wept beside the massive Red Sea. It was You who made a miracle happen to stop Pharaoh and his army of thugs who treated Your people as less than human... and Your mercy to Your own will never be a forgotten gift... as they stood weeping, thinking death was their fate, You opened the seas wide enough and dry enough so Your chosen family could pass from one side to the other escaping the brutality from the Egyptians... then when Pharaoh's military tried the same route, the seas fell upon them drowning each person... sinking as rocks are tossed in the water.. Then as a cloud above this family of Yours, You led them 24 / 7 be it day or night, You were with them.

Then, on Mt. Sinai, You spoke to them, passing onto them, laws You decreed they should abide by, and Moses, your obedient servant, commanded all to obey the Ten Commandments You inscribed on a rock from the mountain.

You gave them bread from heaven to eat and water from a rock to drink. You told them to conquer the land they were headed to as a gift from You, but unfortunately, these ancestors of ours were proud and stubborn and their ears were puffed up because of these flawed characteristics... they said "no" to obeying You and had short memories in the day-to-day miracles You performed on their behalf. They even had the audacity to attempt to appoint a new leader who would march them back to slavery in Egypt.

But because You are a God filled with mercy and forgiveness... who pardons the unpardonable... who gives grace to the undeserving... and who loves the unlovable... yet along with all that... is slow to anger, as shown in Your not simply abandoning them out in the wilderness. Yes, they even had the gall to make a god out of molten gold into a manmade calf, and You still loved them. Their sin was as garbage piled in heaps upon heaps... despite all that, the cloud remained / the food and water did not stop / for forty years You put up with their miserable attitudes, even so far as their clothing and shoes.... in forty years they never wore out.

Next, You battled their wars for them to win, and You put these people in each corner of this land You promised to their ancestors.

King Sihon and King Og gave in to Your power and the land passed onto Your people. Then a massive population took place on this people called Israelites... and it was Your doing. No one had a power greater than You in taking over this land piece by piece. Each nation was simply overwhelmed by Your choice / cities / wells / vineyards / olive orchards / fruit tree acreage / homes already filled with things to live with / were taken over by this promise You made... and Your people were filled with joy from Your hand of giving. But despite all this bounty, again, like their ancestors, rebelled and said "no" to Your laws.

Now they even took it a step further by slaying the prophets You sent to tell them to get back to You... so again, You allowed their enemy to win all the battles and, yet after all this sin, they of course, cry out to You... and being who You are, hear their moaning... and great as You are... with mercy send them saviors who again save them from... not only their enemies, but themselves as well.

Yet, as time moves on... peace settles in ... things are going right... Your own go back to their old ways, and as always, You again have to remind them of their error and allow the enemy success... and yes, they, in time, see the mistakes they have made and cry out, "Save us Lord." You punish... they repent.... time goes by and it happens time and again. Prophets warn them, and for a while they listen, but soon, their memories fade as a cloud in the sky. Yet, in all this time, You don't allow the Israel nation to die, which only show the awesome grace and mercy You possess.

So now, Lord, here we are again. You have kept your promise and we have failed You as our past people have... yet, Lord, this present family of Yours is beset by hardship and struggles which You are totally aware of... Assyria beat us to the ground and your punishment in all our past and present is exactly what it should be... for no matter how good You were to us, we took it for granted and failed miserably to honor and worship You. No matter how much You bless them, they thought... and still think... it all comes from their own hands.

Now Lord, we are slaves here in this land where milk and honey was Your gift to us. We are starving of Your riches on the very land filled with abundance. All those who lord it over us take what You have given to us and use for themselves. Sin has plagued us from the time immortal, Lord. The enemy has power over our lives / our bodies / our land / our cattle / and we serve them as slaves serve their owner and this has caused great misery among Your own nation. Yet, once again, we make a promise to You this day, Lord, "We promise to serve and obey You" and to prove this our princes / priests and Levites put their seal of approval on this promise.

PURPOSE OF PRAYER

Ezra was the top religious leader as the Jews returned from exile. He read to them the laws Moses had written down on scrolls... and after days of reading... praising God... discussing the situation at hand, he prays this prayer on October 10th.

NEHEMIAH 13:14

Oh Lord, please do not forget this good deed... nor Lord, do not forget that I have labored on this temple.

NEHEMIAH 13:22

Recall this good deed, Lord, my God and Savior, and be compassionate on me in agreement with Your fabulous goodness.

NEHEMIAH 13:31

Oh Lord, remember me with all Your kindness.

PURPOSE OF PRAYERS

Nehemiah was trying to put the temple of God back together and difficulty was the word of the day so he prayed these prayers.

JOB

JOB 1:21

I came into this world naked from my mother's womb and when my last breath of earthly air is done, I will possess nothing. All I have came from the hand of the Lord, and all He gave He has the perfect right to take away as well. May God's name be forever blessed.

PURPOSE OF PRAYER

Job was rich in earthly possessions and Satan convinced God to test Job to see if his faith was equal to his words spoken, and after the loss in a short span in time, all Job felt was still blessed by God. So he prayed this prayer.

JOB 7:12-21

Life is a breath of air which describes my being here and nothing... nothing good is left in me. Now you see this figure of a man, yet soon, you will see a corpse for just as a cloud in the sky can surely be seen, yet soon it disappears as if it had never been there... and so it is with humanity. They leave all behind, be it family or home... nothing goes with them.

So please, I ask, let me be honest in my bitterness over what has happened to my soul. Oh Lord, the God of whoever it is I am, what has happened to our relationship? Have I somehow turned into a monstrous sinner and this is how life ends. You are in my dreams / my nightmares / even as I try in vain to forget the misery I lay here in... please, I plead... remove off the face of the earth this so-called human existence I am imprisoned in. My life has no value... none ... so I plead / beg / leave my soul alone as I grieve these last few days I have left in this miserable existence I find myself in.

I ask of you, Lord, what is the value of a person if all You're going to do is place havoc on their life? Must You, Lord, be his accuser day in and day out... testing him 24/7/365. Why not leave the poor creature I am alone to wallow in my final moments of existence... even if it's only a moment to swallow?

Oh Lord, I ask of You, whatever sin I have committed, did it do harm to You the overseer of mankind? What drew You to choose to throw Your wrath at me... and have turned my life upside down? After all, Lord, You have the power to pardon sin, so why not pardon mine, whatever it is I did. Soon, as You well know Lord, this wretched body will lie down and silently You will remove my last breath and death will finally arrive...then when one tries to find me, I will be no more.

PURPOSE OF PRAYER

Job was devastated for all he possessed had been taken away in a moment's time... his riches /his land / his loyalty / his children / his wife's honor / his employer status / gone in a twinkle of an eye... so he prays this prayer to face the inner struggle.

JOB 14:1-21

Oh Lord of all creation, there are but two things... just two... I plead You not to do unto me, and if You agree, then I can at least face You... 1) Don't ever, Lord, abandon me, 2) never allow me to be even near Your presence, yet, Lord, call me and I will be swift as a deer to heed Your call.

How about this, Lord, let me say my piece then You answer.... if that's okay... here are my words. What in the world have I done wrong? What is it that has riled You up? What sin has caused this upheaval in my life? What caused You to turn and walk away from me? What, may I ask, provoked You so that You handed me over to the enemy at hand? I ask of You; do You blame a leaf when it's blown about? Do You go about running after straws that have no value? I feel as a tree rotted within... a coat filled with moth's eating away at it for You have caused me to recall all my history from my youth forward... it's like You have convicted me of a crime I know nothing about... tossed me into a prison to rot my life away and I haven't the foggiest as to why.

Oh Lord, You're well aware of how small a person is in comparison to You. They are here but awhile and in all that time trouble is their shadow... like a flower that blooms in great color for a moment then dies in a short time... as a cloud puts a shadow on earth then within moments, it is gone as if it had never been.

Why Lord, is Your judgment so difficult to bear when humankind is so extremely weak. I ask of You, if one is born impure how can You expect purity of the impure? Oh Lord, You created life, but in doing so, You gave all of it a tiny fraction of time in eternity and not a second more do You add to each one Your gift of life to.... so knowing that, Lord, why not leave them alone... why not peace in that short span of one's life... why not holding back Your anger even if it's warranted.

Yes, Lord, even a tree has hope for it's cut down by the woodsman's axe, but then in a short while it sprouts again... life is renewed and it bursts forth new leaves and new branches... even though deep down its roots are old and its stump looks dead, it has that amazing ability to be reborn, yet when a person dies and is buried beneath the soil... where, Lord, does the spirit end up?

Just as water evaporates or a river disappears... so a person lays down one last time and falls asleep on a permanent bed, but is never to awaken or to be shaken by someone saying, "wake up"... so saying this, Lord, here is my request... Lay me down with the dead and leave me alone until You see fit... Your anger ends against me, but I, as well, ask You this... don't leave me for eternity, no, I ask You to mark on Your calendar when You will say enough is enough."

Yes Lord, it's been said, when one dies one could live again and that thought puts hope within me... so I look to death as a beginning of possibly a new life. You would whisper, "Come" and I would run to Your side and then You would say, "Well done." But as for now, the time at hand, this moment... You have set the stage, and as I walk across it, You point out every error I make... every mistake is noted and soon You created a book of errors against me.

Oh Lord, the mountains of earth wear out and over time disappear. Water constantly grinds on a rock so it, as well, disappears. Flood waters tear at the land and it disappears. So it is with this created humankind. His hopes are dashed by Your anger and so as day turns to night, they are gone / old / wrinkled / aged / off to the land of the dead, not knowing if his past will be recalled by the future... never knowing if their offspring succeed or fail at life. Only two things remain-sorrow and grief.

PURPOSE OF PRAYER

Job is unhappy God has decided to punish him as he sees no reason to be punished. He claims innocence by the standards he preached day in and day out so he takes his reasoning to God in this prayer.

PSALMS

PSALMS

The Book of Psalms is a prayer journal from Chapter 1 through Chapter 150. I, the writer, have chosen *ten* of David's prayers to God. It's my hope you will walk through the pages of God's Holy Word to find a prayer that fits the situation you are walking through for David faced many a trial, but he depended solely on God to defend him no matter what the enemy or what the struggle was. You and I can do the same. Prayer is our only way of communicating with the Creator of all that is.

PSALM 23:1-6

The Lord is my Shepherd, He provides all my needs. He made the meadows and the grass so I may find rest in Him. He walks with me beside the quiet streams and puts within me the inner strength. He knows what I need. He whispers to me to honor and obey Him. Yes, even though the Valley of Death sits before me, His care will keep fear away as we walk side by side, one with another. As my enemies watch, You sit me at Your table of honor, filled with foods so delicious to even eat, for You have allowed me to be a guest in Your home. All my days, Your kindness and goodness shall follow me as a shadow follows a deer... and when my journey is over, Your home shall be my home.

PURPOSE OF PRAYER

David was stating his faith in the God who had saved him / blessed him and promised him safety on his journey to eternity with him.

PSALMS 32:1-11

What joy lies within those who have been forgiven? What wonders when sin has been buried? What spiritual fortunes for those who have confessed to God the errors they made and God has erased the sin. Yes, I admit Lord, in past times, I would not utter the words, "I am a sinner," but in doing that, misery found a way to rob me of peace and because of that lie within me, Your grasp on my soul was heavy. I had not an ounce of power from such a force as Yours, yet finally, I gave up and simply admitted my sinful nature and the lying stopped. You forgave... I was free from such stupidity. Guilt flew out the window as a bird escapes from a cage.

Wisdom says, "Confession of sin cleanses the soul, and I yell out, "Yes," in agreement. It is You, Lord, who hides me from the storms of life. It is You, Lord, who keeps trouble at bay. It is You who shadows me. I listen... You speak, saying, "Follow the path I have made for you and your walk will be smoother than a horse without a bridle or a mule that has no master to lead it." You can be sure of this... sorrow always follows the unbeliever, yet the opposite is true for the believer... for trust in God brings peace. Shout to the heavens that God has put within you the path to obedience which brings joy to the heart.

PURPOSE OF PRAYER

David is admitting without God on his side, he is a loser before the game starts.

PSALM 39:1-3

"Quit complaining," I said to myself, so quietness sealed my lips and especially when those around me do not believe in You, Lord. Yet as I stood, not speaking... I could feel this turmoil within me wanting to burst open and the longer I fumed the hotter within I got until at last the words spilled out, "Oh Lord, help me to not fail or forget life is short." No longer than the arm I stretch out. To You life is a moment in eternity's clock... yes, proud / frail... a shadow rushing from sun up to sun down, all without value, piling up wealth so the heirs can spend it.

Oh Lord, You're my only hope... save me from the grasp of sin for its long arm reaches out to overpower me. Yes, I admit the punishment You give is always fair and just and deserving for when You pass judgment, who has the ability to escape.

It is a fact of life, Lord, humankind is as fragile as a moth eaten coat and as weak as a breath of air. So Lord, hear me... listen please... see my tears for I am but on a journey passing through time as all my fathers were before me. Oh Lord, put within me the ability to recover so that joy and happiness can once again visit before You send the angel of death.

PURPOSE OF PRAYER

David knew God was the only One who could renew what he had temporarily lost so he prayed God would again restore him to vitality.

PSALMS 49:5-20

With the Lord on your side there is never a need to fear when trouble arrives at your door... even if you're surrounded 360° by your enemies. Your enemies trust in all their wealth / their power... and they even boast of such, yet not one can save themselves or another from the penalty that must be paid for sin.

Understand that God forgives, but it cannot be bought. The soul God implants into the human spirit is far too precious to be bought and sold by such earthly means as gold and silver for if one could gather all of those materials up in one large sum, it wouldn't come close to the value of just one soul.

All must die, be you rich / powerful / proud / wise ... no one escapes this final conclusion of life, and no, the poor / widow / orphan / slave... does not escape this finality as well. All one possesses in earthly goods is left behind for others to spend or give away or use at their discretion... as one dead cannot tell the living how to live. Yet one goes around accumulating estates as though you would live forever.

Yet, just as the world of the animal kingdom... who all die... so does humankind. And, as foolish as it sounds, these who possess such great wealth will be recalled as having great wisdom, yet they had not enough wisdom to seek a way to save their souls. Yes, the Shepherd of all humankind is death, and as morning, the rich will serve the poor... the evil will wait upon the good... for all the pomp / wealth is lost at death, as it can no longer hide the evilness that lies within humankind. But as for me, the God I serve will redeem my soul from the angel of death, for God will open his door to eternity and say, "Welcome."

So I tell you, don't be frustrated when the rich get richer and live in estates built for many, yet only a few live in them... for at death time, the estate stays and they leave. It can be said of the rich that their lives seemed joyous and un-wanting, yet at death, who recalls all their earthly goods, and even though they may have had great applause from the living, death, to them, will only bring silence for eternity.

PURPOSE OF PRAYER

David prayed this prayer to give hope for the down and out / the lost / the hopeless / the addicted ... that they, because of God, can have the thought they can be cared for... their only reliance is God – not money or power.

PSALM 63:1-11

Oh Lord, You know how I search for You. How I thirst after You in a land where water is unable to be found. Oh, how I long to locate You, Lord. How I would give anything to be in Your sanctuary and there, see Your power and glory. For Lord, it can be said in truth, Your love and kindness are greater than the gift of life itself. Oh, how joyous I am in praising Your name. I will honor and bless You for as long as the life You put within me. My hands are lifted in prayer and with that You put within me, contentment.

Yes Lord, I praise You even in lying awake at night... my thoughts are of You... how You have protected and helped me... how You have hidden me under Your wings... as an eagle hides its young. Your power protects my daily journey, yet You are well aware of those who would laugh at my demise, and yes, their day of reckoning is at hand, for soon the angel of death shall take them to their place of judgment for eternity. Yes, rejoice in the Lord... and liars be silent.

PURPOSE OF PRAYER

David was hounded by thugs who would kill him if Satan had his way, but he knew who was in charge of all mankind, be they good or evil. David never doubted God and he prayed this way.

PSALMS 73:1-8

God makes it a point to be good to Israel, and to those whose hearts are pure within their being. Yet, for me, I came too close to falling off a dangerous cliff. If not for God, most assuredly, the fall would have taken place. For I was envious of those who had more than I. I was envious of those who snubbed their nose at God because of their fame, they thought it was A-Okay… yet, had they known it would cause them what they are headed for, surely they would have stayed silent.

These folks of prominence have lives that are seemingly un-frustrated / non-anxiety / no problems to deal with… so they exhibit this in the lifestyle they live. They want for nothing because in their minds they have it all… they laugh as if You, Lord, didn't exist… and they treat those who have faith in You as less than human… they act as if they created themselves and will build their own heaven after their last breath of air… and seeing this Your people are confused as they take in all they see and hear, and ask the question, "Does God see? Does He hear? Does it not bother Him that these are arrogant human beings, who seemingly could care less if He were alive or dead. For they have all they need so they yell out… who needs God. They live in the richest homes / eat the best foods / and problems evade them like a storm that never materialized.

Are we, the children of God, wrong in our faith by believing as we do? It seems trouble is all we face day in and day out. Yes, you can be sure I would have betrayed the very people You call Your own, had I believed all that was said by Your own. Easy to explain this seemingly complex scenario? No… but this I can say to those who curse God for whatever reason… One day, on the Lord's clock… one day when the angel of death arrives at the front door of arrogance… at that moment… in a split second… at the twinkle of an eye… God will put arrogance to bed, and God, as swift as an eagle catches its prey, send these ungodly souls to their eternal judgment. Then where will all the riches be / the fine homes

/ the big parties / they will awake in total darkness and deafening silence and not able to speak a word as their mouths have been closed by God.

At seeing all this, fear struck me instantly as I saw my stupidity at my envy / my ignorance at my jealousy... and I felt as if I had betrayed You, Lord, because of this inner conflict... But even in all this, thank You for assuring me You love me and hold onto me as an eagle clings to its young. Your wisdom and counsel is far greater than any mere accumulation of earthly wealth. Yes Lord, I look to the day You say, "Welcome," for who do I have but You to save me from all my earthly sins and errors. Yes Lord, my health may fail / my faith may falter / my riches may dwindle to poverty / yet, in all that, You remain. You're my strength, Lord. But a warning to those who turn their backs to God. It will be a poor decision... one that will cost a heavenly home lost. Don't serve another god, instead revere Jehovah.... and as for me, you can be sure, I stay as close to God as the clothing I wear. I choose You, Lord, and will tell all who will listen of this eternal decision.

PURPOSE OF PRAYER

David was hearing reports that envy and jealousy were within the Israeli family because some had more than others in worldly goods, and those with less were angry at God for such... so he prayed this prayer.

PSALM 90:1-12

Before anything was created, Israel was Your family, Lord, for You are God... no beginning and no ending. You speak and creation begins and ends. A word to the angel of death, and in a moment's notice, a human's life is gone forever, never to be seen again. A thousand years plus a thousand are but a twinkle of an eye to You / a nanosecond... yet mankind goes through this journey thinking life will be forever, and yet, as quick as it got here will be as quick as it leaves. Like grass that is mowed down not to be recalled.

Oh Lord, Your anger upon us is more than the human spirit can bear. Your wrath, simply put, overwhelms us as You write out our sins one at a time. All the known ones, and all those hidden in the deep, dark spaces in our hearts and souls that You see as if one pointed a light beam at them. So, acknowledging that, we simply give in knowing we are no match to Your awesome power. Yes, it's said seventy years a life is given and some even to eighty, yet if one lives to these lengths, what value were these to the journey... emptiness and pain have been the road traveled. So Lord, my prayer is this... teach us to number our days / or years... in order to recognize how short life is and perhaps, by doing so, we can say at the journey's end, it had value.

PURPOSE OF PRAYER

David knew God only gave humankind a certain amount of time for each to live out a life. This prayer was to bring to the attention of making each life have value especially if the life was zeroed in on God.

PSALMS 112:1-10

For all who fear God and trust Him without doubt, praise the Lord. Those who, with pure hearts put their full faith in God are blessed beyond what can be said here... and happy is the person who awakes eager to do God's will during their daily journey. This person's children will be greatly honored for a parent's children who obey the Lord are a special bond to the Lord, and this person who makes it a point to have God as a companion 24/7 shall see wealth in numerous ways and they will not be forgotten as a leaf blown in the wind. When trouble arrives at their front door they ask God to answer it. Kindness and mercy to these are as a light to a candle and it can be said with confidence that life is good for they have learned the secret of doing business in an ethical manner... such individuals are not overtaken by evilness.

Your care of them, Lord, is as evident as a sunrise. Yes Lord, when bad news arrives these faithful do not stand around in fear and dread for they are confident within their minds and souls, God, You Lord, are with them and will not depart under any circumstances. This is the sole reason why they don't live in fear of what happened yesterday / today or what tomorrow holds... they give, give and give knowing well their return by God is multiplied over and over and over... yes evilness sits by madder than a hot head that God's protection is so evident by the lives they lead.

PURPOSE OF PRAYER

David had God's courage within him and now he was praying others could catch it to share it as well.

PSALMS 139:1-24

Oh Lord, there isn't a thing You are not aware of in my humanity. Head to foot and all in between. My thoughts / my intentions / my past / present / future, and because of You, I can rest assured the path You're leading me on is the will You have for my life. Not a nanosecond am I out of your sight. Even the words I am about to speak, You know before they leave my mouth.

You have blessed me far greater than imagination could have predicted. It is too glorious to take in. Thank you, Your spirit is with me 24 / 7 / 365 and never can I be without You...never. If I were to go to hell, You would be with me. If I could come to heaven, You would be with me. If I traveled to the farthest corners of earth, there You would be with me. It is You, Lord.

You alone who guides me... strengthens me... and yet for reasons unknown... if I try to hide in a cave, You're with me. If I try some dark, remote place, You turn my light on... for You Lord, darkness and light are as equal as the sun rising and falling. Yes Lord, thank You, every part of my humanity was woven together by Your so delicate hands... which when thought of is too wonderful / too complex to even remotely comprehend.

At the time I was conceived / in the innermost part of my mother, You were there with me. During that time of dark seclusion, You watched me develop. Each moment was recorded in Your book of life. It is a glorious thing to know by faith, Lord, that I am on Your mind this very moment and have been since I was conceived, and will be till You call me home. Such a wonderful thought is far above my human ability to take in.

And yet Lord, in all this You are well aware of the evilness of humankind. You as well know their thoughts / intentions / deeds for wrongness, and will, on your timetable, deal with each one according to the lives they led. Yes Lord, these enemies of Yours are as well enemies of mine, but even in this Lord, I plead with You, spare me Lord / test me / and if You find me to not be exactly as You want me, then You straighten me out. You put me on Your path, You create in me a desire to be as You would have me and lead me to You, Lord.

PURPOSE OF PRAYER

David had become so aware of how God worked in his humanity that he shared it in this prayer.

PSALM 141:1-10

Oh Lord, tears fill my eyes and flow down my face like a river flows over rocks embedded in the sand below it. Listen, Lord, as I cry out to You. Take this prayer as a living sacrifice to Your holy name. Help me Lord, please. Seal my lips before they say words You would not have me speak. Seal my heart from the lust it desires. Seal my soul from intentions to do evil. Keep my feet from wanting to run with sinners. Take me home, Lord, if I am to be as the ungodly.

And if I am to be reprimanded for a wrong action on my part, because of wrong action, then let it be so. Yet Lord, teach me to be in constant prayer / constant gratitude. Allow me Lord, the ability to be as You want me, so others can see it's the right way to be. Oh Lord, You are my rock, my rescuer, my hope, so keep me safe, Lord, in the palm of Your hand. Allow the wicked to get their just due.

PURPOSE OF PRAYER

David was in pain over his current circumstances and reached out in faith to the God who had sustained him all his life.

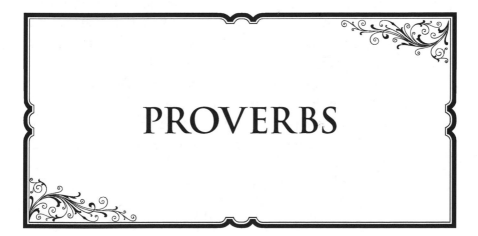

PROVERBS

PROVERBS 30:1-9

Oh Lord, I am ready to come home... tired / worn out / and distraught enough to even admit I am not part of the human race. Humankind, Lord, bewilders me... and yes, You Lord, as well confound me for who but You can go from earth to heaven. Who but You, tells the winds when to blow or stay silent. Who but You says to the oceans stop and it obeys. Who, Lord, but You could have created all that there is. No one is like You... and even the Son You have; his name is blinded to us.

You are truth, Lord, as every word that is spoken by You proves it so. You defend those who pant after Your will for their lives. Oh Lord, I ask you two things to allow to occur during this journey... First help my lips to never to lie under any circumstance. Second, never allow me to live in poverty nor in riches. Simply, keep me content with what You have provided, for Lord, if I were to become rich, I might forget who gave it to me, and if I become poor, I may resort to thievery and this would insult Your holy name.

PURPOSE OF PRAYER

This was written to share with God his power and our poverty being dependent on him for all our life trials and triumphs.

ISAIAH

ISAIAH 25:1-7

You, Lord, are an awesome God who knows how to put together wonderments beyond human abilities. Praise Your name, Lord. You planned them before the earth was formed... You set them in motion on Your time frame. You have that ability. Only You could turn a robust city into a heap of rubble. Forts made not to fall into ruins. Great buildings designed by humankind, not to fall... yet a word from You, and they tumble as a rock falls off a mountain.

Let nations who hear this tremble in fear of Your mighty power and those nations who treat its own with ruthless power... may they come to their knees in obeying Your word and glorifying Your name. Yet, Lord, take pity on the poor and be a shelter for them. Allow the palm of Your hand to protect them. And may You put a shield around them from those who would take advantage of them, and Lord, may I beg You, cool the heated temperament of those nations who would rule with fist of iron if given the power.

PURPOSE OF PRAYER

Isaiah speaks of the richness of God on all humankind, but especially on those who put their trust in him.

ISAIAH 26:10-19

Oh, how the wicked love their wickedness, not even taking a moment in time to notice the mercy You show them... for their wickedness has made them blind to Your goodness. They plug up their ears if You even hint at judgment. They go blind if You raise Your fist to their punishment. And yet, Lord, I ask You even in this blasphemy, show them the great love You have for your own and just maybe, maybe they will awake to see Your goodness to them, and it will shame them into changing their ways. Allow within them, the same fire that burns within their enemies.

Oh Lord, may peace fall upon us as a gentle shower falls from the heavens for all we have, even life itself, is a gift from You, and yes, we are at fault for worshiping other gods, but we have come to our senses and now worship only You... for the gods of past have died and left, not to return to haunt us with their evil desires. It was You who slain them... and it was You who buried them. Praise the Lord... for it is He who has created and made Israel what it is and has taken its borders and moved them to create an even larger nation. Oh Lord, Your own look to You, especially when all other roads have been blocked off... and when You laid a punishment on them, a whispered prayer went to Your home.

Oh Lord, how we miss your presence among us. We are in suffering, Lord, as a woman about to give birth cries and weeps in the pain upon her, and yet in time, relief will come to her... yet to us, none is in sight. All our efforts to grab Your attention have been unheard, and yet Lord, we can rejoice even in this for we know who protects us, and to those who put their faith in You, shall rise even if buried deep down... for one day the dust shall return to the living and the voices will sing hallelujah for Your remembrance of their commitment to You. Like dew falling from the heavens, so Your mercy will fall upon them.

PURPOSE OF PRAYER

Isaiah was sent to tell King Hezekiah to put his life's results in order for God was taking him home... but the king wept openly, saying this prayer in order that God would have mercy, and just maybe, grant him a bit more time at living life.

ISAIAH 38:3

Oh, God of heaven and earth, please recall my faithfulness to You and as well my obedience to every word You have spoken to me.

PURPOSE OF PRAYER

Isaiah is pleading to God to have mercy upon his own choosing knowing full well all the punishment thrown down from heaven was well deserved, but he asks, "How long until your temper is quieted."

ISAIAH 64:1-12

Oh, Lord, what's to hold You back from walking the dusty roads of this creation of Yours. How the earth would shake in fear. Your glory would set the forest ablaze... Your being here would boil the oceans to absolute dryness... nations would stand in awe. The enemy would know them... why they are able to triumph. The world seeks a God as You as one looking for a lost nugget of gold, and yet Your mercy on Your own, is far greater than all the gold the earth contains.

You are a God who opens Your door to those who pant after Your will, and yet Lord, the truth is, we... Your own... are ungodly. Sinners of the greatest depth – so Your punishment is just and fair, and I ask Lord, how is it You even think of us, let alone save us. Whereas, infected with sin as an animal is infected with a disease, we wear robes to honor ourselves and they turn to filthy rags. So like the seasons come and go, we do as well, and our sins follow us like a shadow from the sun.

We forget to even call upon You when trials knock at our door. So doing what's right for such thinking, You turn your back to us which we deserve to have done. But even with this disease-infected thinking, You stay as our father. We are the child, You are the honored father all born into Your family, so knowing that Lord, forgive our shortcomings. Forget those sins that tear at us 24/7... look upon us as Your own choosing. It is true Lord, the cities You built lie in ruins. Jerusalem is a wilderness.

Your temple is burned unrecognizable. The beauty within them is as dust. And after all this punishment upon a people who deserve it, will You continue to have a deaf ear to our pleadings. Will Your silence haunt us? Will Your punishment not have an end?

PURPOSE OF PRAYER

Isaiah, as per his entire sixty-six chapters, deals with the human characteristics - be they good or evil. He, in his time, was the prophet of God and spoke what the Lord put within him to say to those who needed to hear it.

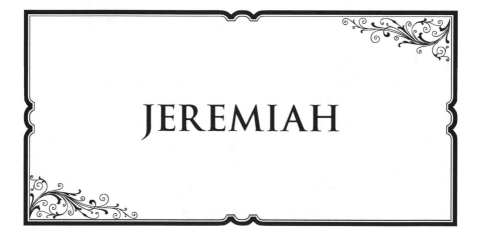

JEREMIAH

JEREMIAH 10:6-10

My God, my God, there is no God as You are. Your greatness is unmatchable. Your name has power the human intellect cannot comprehend, so I ask Lord, who would dare to consider not to fear You. You are the King of kings and in all creation... all the wisest... all the brightest... all put together cannot compare to Your wisdom as there is no one like You, Lord. No one.

The fool worships a god he created with his own hands. Silver from Tarshish... Gold from Uphaz. Give it to a skilled craftsman and all of a sudden an idol to worship... and to add insult to their foolishness, they have clothing made by experts to make them think they are wise in their foolishness. Yet Lord, You are the only God to worship and honor. The God who lives.... the God who had no past and no future, for You have always been and will always be. May the earth You created tremble in fear and hide in the palm of Your hand, at Your anger, at the fools who sin in pleasure.

PURPOSE OF PRAYER

Jeremiah was desperate as he had thought that since all had abandoned him for whatever reason, God might as well.

JEREMIAH 10:23-24

Oh, the God of my soul. It is well known humankind does not have the power to map out tomorrow today. So, Lord, I ask You, please correct me if I am out on the wrong course... and as well, Lord, be kind to my spirit. Don't correct me with Your anger, Lord, for if You were to do so... surely death would knock at my door.

PURPOSE OF PRAYER

Jeremiah told both the wisest and the leaders of their sin against God, and he as well, knew the consequences of such statements.

JEREMIAH 11:20

Oh, Lord, the God of all creation, You are just and fair in all circumstances... yet I plead with You... Look into the hearts and minds of these men... read their motives... write down their intentions, then repay them Lord, for the plans they have made, plotting out evil. I look to You and only You for true justice.

PURPOSE OF PRAYER

Jeremiah is sickened by the hearts and minds of those who surrounded him, and so he pleads with God for justice.

JEREMIAH 12:1-6

Oh, Lord, justice is Your nature, for You have shown that in the cases I have laid before You... and now I have a statement / a question / a complaint, Lord. Why is it... and I beg You to tell me... The wicked seem to prosper far greater than the good? Those who outwardly prove they are of an evil nature seem so happy and content versus those who run after your obedience? My confusion lies in that You give them life... they age... and as rotten as they are, whatever business they tackle, it grows in multiples? And they laugh all the way to the bank... they even have the audacity to yell out, "thank god"... yet You well know, it's not You they are thanking, it's the god they created within their own hearts.

Yet Lord, You know me as one would know their own name, and You know my loyalty... yet, Lord, I am as poor as mice. So I ask You, please do to them as one would do to a sheep about to be slaughtered for sacrifice. Judge them, Lord, as only You know how, fair and just. I have to ask, Lord, how long will You put up with such as You see going on? For the grass even has a season before it withers and dies. The people, Lord, who chase after good are bewildered and even the wild animals have left in disgust of these sins for they yell out in the streets for all to hear, including You, "God doesn't care and if He did, what's He to do about it... we are safe without worry."

PURPOSE OF PRAYER

Jeremiah prays on behalf of the Israeli people. For God has them mourning as business has stopped cold in its tracks / water is no longer in the wells / rain has disappeared / farmers fear for the future / grass has ceased to grow. Jeremiah prays about this illness God has laid upon the land and his own.

JEREMIAH 14:7-9

Oh, Lord, let not your reputation be soiled because of the multiple sins we have made in error against You. You, Lord, are our only hope here in this land You gifted to our forefathers, called Israel. Trouble to You is opportunity, and yet, Lord, when that disease of trouble falls upon us, Your voice stays silent.

Is it because You no longer care for us, Lord? Are You without an answer for our situation? Are You still, Lord, able to save us, especially from ourselves... and yet, Lord, even though I say all that, I know You're here. We are your creation / your family / your people / so my prayer is simple... Lord, don't leave us no matter how great our sins pile up.

PURPOSE OF PRAYER

Jeremiah sees the plight of the Israeli people so he prays mightily that God would again forgive them and bless them.

JEREMIAH 14:19-22

The people wail, Lord, crying over the question, "Has God forgotten us?" "Is Jerusalem no longer your city?" "Will punishment bring peace?" All are asking / questioning / begging for an answer, Lord, and yet You may heal outward problems, but what of our inward problems, Lord, they are the worst of the two. If we confess our father's sins, will You favor us with forgiveness? If we confess our father's sins, will you heal us?

Oh, God, the awfulness of Your hate and anger towards us is greater than one can bear. Oh, Lord of all, for Your namesake, don't allow yourself to not follow through on the promises You have made to this people of Yours... for I ask You, Lord, who but You can provide rain. Certainly a god made with human hands is not a god, therefore, is unable to do anything but be still. Oh, Lord, we wait upon You. Help us for You are a God of mercy.

PURPOSE OF PRAYER

Jeremiah was looking for a way out of the dilemma he found himself in, knowing that his one and only solution was prayer.

JEREMIAH 15:15-18

I suffer, Lord, for your sake. I am persecuted because I have shouted Your name to those who had ears to hear and to those who wouldn't listen. My plea is this: don't give them, Lord, the opportunity to kill this body You created. You rescue me now. Pay them back for such plans. You, Lord, sustain me. Your words are my food / my joy / my delight. Even in my darkest moment they are as torches bearing light.

Oh, Lord, I am proud to be a witness to Your name for as You can well see, I refrain from the parties / the festivals. I sit with You next to me holding me as a father holds a son. And yet, Lord, the sins of the people disgust me as it does You. Don't, Lord, leave me to be persecuted by such evil for, as You know, if You don't stop them, who am I to call upon. Yet Lord, I am well aware, Your help comes in two ways... one is as a floodgate opens for water to flow, and two, is as a barren desert dry as a bone.

PURPOSE OF PRAYER

Jeremiah was being threatened / cursed / talked about / rumors were on the streets... so he did what prophets do... he prayed.

JEREMIAH 18:19-23

Save me, Lord, as You have the heavenly eyes to see their intentions. I ask, Lord, should evil override good? What, Lord, have I said to have them set traps for me to fall prey to? I have told them of You, Lord, and now they hate me for doing so. So knowing this about them, Lord, would You please allow their own to starve to death... let the sword spill their blood... allow their wives to be widows and to be barren in the womb... allow epidemics to fall upon their homes... let their young die on the battlefield.

Allow, Lord, the enemy success in capturing them. They have made plans to kill me... now turn the tables on them, Lord. Hear it all... so don't, Lord, forgive their wickedness. You see that they die on Your clock of time. Let Your anger lay on them, Lord.

PURPOSE OF PRAYER

Jeremiah was down in the dumps as those who thought they were the righteous looked upon Jeremiah, God's prophet, as a fool who had lost his mind and treated him as such.

JEREMIAH 20:12-18

Oh, Lord, the Creator of all there is, who but You knows a righteous heart? Who but You, Lord, has that awesome ability to look into the heart and mind to examine it for its thoughts and deeds? Oh, Lord, allow Your vengeance of terror to fall upon these who harm me for speaking what You have told me to say... for my only cause to do so is committed to You. Therefore, let my voice sing out to You, Lord. Praise Him for it is He and He alone who has delivered me. Yes, poor and in need from those who oppress me.

Yes, may the day I was born be cursed. Cursed may the man be who said to my father, a son has been born to you. And yes, let that man who took that news to my father be destroyed as those cities God has, in past days, desolated without an ounce of mercy. Put fear within him... all this because instead of bearing good news to my father, he should have taken the sword to kill me at birth. Yes, Lord, why not have me killed during those months within my mother's womb and allow that to be my grave. Why, Lord, was I born / conceived; my life to this moment has been nothing but trouble / sorrow / shame.

PURPOSE OF PRAYER

The Lord told Jeremiah to buy a certain field... pay for it... do it in front of witnesses... and knowing full well the enemy of Israel was knocking at the front door of the city Jeremiah prayed over.

JEREMIAH 32:17-25

Oh, Lord, You and You alone made the heavens and the earth by that power only You possess, Lord. Nothing is too difficult for You... nothing. You, Lord, are loving and kind to multitudes, and yet children must suffer for the great sins of their fathers. You, Lord, are the great God of all, mighty in power... Your wisdom is beyond humankind's ability to remotely comprehend. Only You, Lord, can perform the miracles You do. Your eyes look onto the souls of humankind and reward or punish each one for the life they led and the deeds they have done.

In Egypt, Your miracles are still discussed today as if they happened yesterday. And yes, Lord, today in Israel Your miraculous hand of miracles is still working its way through this land as well as the entire world You created and Your name, Lord, is great in eons past and this very day. You saved Israel in the coming out of Egypt. You gave freely this land You promised our forefathers... a land that flows with all the goodness You promised them. You handed the enemy to Israel so they could live in peace upon it.

Yet, Lord, in all that giving, the people have refused to obey Your laws. They have hidden Your laws so they can yell out, "No one told us" ... and this is why You have punished us. See the ramps built up against the city walls as Babylon will conquer by sword / famine / disease... and it's all come to pass exactly as You said it would and determined it would. Oh, Lord, then tell me why it is You want me to buy this field, paying good money for such and doing so in front of witnesses, and Lord, knowing all along this city will soon belong to our enemies.

PURPOSE OF PRAYER

Jeremiah prophesied the fall of Jerusalem and weeps over its destruction.

LAMENTATIONS

LAMENTATIONS 2:20-22

Oh, Lord, please take a moment and think about your resolve... these are Your people / Your creation. You are going to allow this to Your own, Lord. I ask, shall the mothers eat their own children, those who they bore and raised? Shall the priest and prophets die within Your temple, Lord? You see them lying in the streets dead / old / young / girls / boys / all killed by the enemy of Israel by sword, and Lord, You killed them... Your anger...Your mercy has run from Israel, leaving the dead to rot in the open. You called for destruction and You got what was delivered. None have escaped... none remain... all lay dead on the streets of Your city, looked upon by Israel's enemy.

PURPOSE OF PRAYER

Jeremiah prophesies the fall of Jerusalem and weeps over its destruction.

LAMENTATIONS 3:43-66

Oh, Lord, Your anger engulfs us. You have slain us without mercy. You have, Lord, put a cloud between us so that our prayers do not go to Your ear. You, Lord, have made us the garbage pit among the nations. We are the bottom of the rung. Our enemies yell at us enough so that fear fills our hearts and we are trapped with not a way of escape even if one tried. Oh, Lord, the tears that fall upon my face are as waves pounding a beach, all because of this, Your own destruction.

Now I beg You, Lord, take a moment and peek down upon this sorrow that lays upon me like a wet blanket... my heart is broken, Lord, seeing what is happening to the young women of Jerusalem. The enemy chases us, Lord, as one would chase after a bird. This enemy You allowed in here threw me in a well and capped its top and the water in the well was as high as my head, and above, I thought for sure You had called me home. Life was over, I simply assumed, but by your awesome mercy, I cried out to You in desperation and You heard my fearful plea. You saw my weeping even with water above my head, and even in that despair, Lord, You spoke and said, "Do not fear."

Oh, God, what a lawyer You are... for who else would I call upon but You to plead my case. You, Lord, saved me from the wrongdoers. You are my judge and jury, prove me correct, Lord. You hear the name calling against me... the accusations / the whispering / the gossip / the rumors / their laughter / and they have the gall to sing, thinking they have heard my last words... But, I say, Lord, repay evil for evil. Do unto them as they would have done unto me. Hard are their hearts, so hard a rod cannot break them. Chase them / catch them / destroy them so their names are not even mentioned in the history books of time.

PURPOSE OF PRAYER

Jeremiah begs for mercy from God and vengeance on Israel's enemies.

LAMENTATIONS 5:1-22

Oh Lord, please don't fail to forget all the misery that has fallen upon us. Look, Lord, at the sorrow we lay in with our nation occupied and filled with non-Israelis / foreigners / which, Lord, has left us as orphans. Our fathers dead / our mothers widowed... even the water that flows, we are forced to pay for. The fuel we need, we are charged more than the rate all others pay.

Our necks, Lord, are bowed to our enemy's feet as we work seemingly 24/7/365 for wages less than all others. We must beg both Egypt and Assyria for the simplest of foods being bread at minimum. Yes, Lord, our fathers sinned and have died at Your judgment of them, yet now we suffer still for what sins they committed... and even our former servants, Lord, have become our masters. Who will save us, Lord, if not You. We even sneak out in the night to hunt food, knowing well... if caught... death is the penalty for such an act.

Our skin turned black from such horrendous famine. The Jewish women are raped from Jerusalem to the outer cities You gave our forefathers. Even the young girls are seduced at the enemy's will. Princes are hung by their thumbs / elderly treated as less than human / young men enslaved at grinding their grain / and young boys stagger under the load they must carry. No longer do the city's men sit at the gates to the town's entrance / no longer do the young dance and sing / joy has fled as a wild goat runs from its owner / dancing has turned to a death song / the glory is gone / the crown has fallen, and our sins have caused this to be / our hearts are weak with a sickness that has no cure / our eyes weep with sorrow / Jerusalem and God's temple are as empty as a hole with nothing in it / wild animals run about as if they were the landlords.

Oh, Lord, in all this woe, You remain always the same... generation to generation... Your wisdom continues. Will You, Lord, forget us forever? Will You forsake us from here on out? You, Lord, have the power to turn us back to being that which You created us to be. This is our only hope / our only means to joy again... or Lord, have we sinned so great Your rejection will continue for generations ahead. Are You, Lord, still angry at us?

PURPOSE OF PRAYER

Jeremiah realizes what a predicament Israel has put itself in while not thinking God would allow punishment on His chosen family. Yet, He does, and Jeremiah is attempting to appease God with tears of sorrow for such stupidity.

EZEKIEL

EZEKIEL 4:14

Oh Lord, my God, must I, Lord... must I be put into the lap of sin by using the excrement of an animal... as never in my life, even as a child, have I ever, Lord, eaten an animal that has died of some type of illness or even one that I found lame or dead... never, Lord... You would know, Lord, any animal that is absolutely forbidden to eat by the law set down, I have held myself against doing.

PURPOSE OF PRAYER

Ezekiel, the prophet, was following every detail the Lord laid upon him, and he balked at this one and this only, and God allowed him his request.

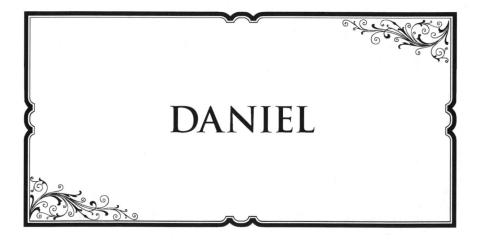

DANIEL

DANIEL 2:20-23

Blessed be the name of God forever in all eternity for His name is wonderful. He and He alone has all the wisdom and power. All is under His complete control, be it earth's nations and all its powers and events. Kings come and go at His choosing. Wisdom is a gift from Him and He sets it upon those whom He chooses. Intelligence is a gift given by His will.

Hidden mysteries blinded to mankind are revealed to those He chooses to give such insight to... nothing is hidden to Him for the darkest of dark is like a light has been turned on. He has no obstacles. Yes, I thank Him / I praise Him... Oh God, of all my forefathers, thank You for instilling into me this wisdom / the health I am in, I am in awe of, and visions of king's dreams with the understanding of what those dreams mean.

PURPOSE OF PRAYER

Daniel is given the ability by God to read with understanding one dream King Nebuchadnezzar has and he thanks God for it.

DANIEL 9:4-19

Oh, Lord, You are an awesome God. Never, ever do You break a promise to those who love You and obey every law You have set before them. Yet, Lord, our sins are piled above our heads. Our rebellion is worse than worse... we have buried your laws and thrown dirt upon its grave. We plug our ears to Your prophet's words spoken by You to reach us. You have sent prophet after prophet telling kings / princes / ordinary people how they should live out their lives.

Yes, Lord, you are righteous.... but we are dirt of the ground. Sinners in the past, and sinners this moment. None of us are free from this crime of sin... none. Judah's people / Jerusalem citizens / all of Israel and all those You have driven away from Israel... all are guilty of turning our backs to You as if You didn't create us. The weight of this guilt on all is heavy as the largest mountain in Israel and shame fills our humanity Lord... but for our sake Your mercy is far greater than our sinful nature and Your pardon greater than our guilt.

Yes, Lord, we are sinners from birth until death. We pay no attention to Your laws You passed down through Your prophets of time. None in Israel is free from this crime against You.... none. The impact upon us as a nation, Lord, is severe just as You told Moses it would be. All has come to pass upon us and we are deservingly treated so... Moses' words ring true. Never, Lord, in all of Israel's history has such a disaster fallen upon its people in Jerusalem, be they kings or the ordinary citizen. All the curses Moses wrote out have come to fruition / the hardships / all the worst of the worse has been laid on us as a carpet is laid on a floor / and yet with all this misery our stubborn nature still refuses to bend our knee, and even if that miracle were to happen, it would not come close to satisfying Your anger against us.

And now, because of our rebellion, Lord, You have simply put into action what You said You would do eons ago / and is the Lord fair in His action against us? Yes. It was You, Lord, who saved us from the slavery of Egypt / so now we ask You, do it once again. Yes, we are sinners, but Your mercy is far greater than our sins, Lord, so turn Your anger from Jerusalem, please. This is Your city / Your holy mountain / and You can surely hear the enemy of Israel mock us as we lay in ruins for our sins. Hear this servant's prayer.

Listen, Lord, as I beg of You, allow Your face to once again shine with joy and peace upon this sanctuary built to honor You. Do this, for You Lord / bend down Your ear / hear my whispers / open Your eyes and see our blatant sins / see this city of Yours lay in ruins for the world knows it is Yours. Yes, Lord, we are not asking You to help us because we deserve it / we are asking You to be merciful to a sinful nation. Hear me, Lord / act upon this prayer. Don't even hesitate to start. For Your sake, open this nation of people You own as is shown in Your name upon this city.

PURPOSE OF PRAYER

Daniel learns from the prophet Jeremiah that Israel must lay in ruins for seventy years for its sins of the past and present so he pleads Israel's case.

JONAH

JONAH 2:2-9

I am in a great deal of trouble and I cried out to God and by His mercy He answered me. From the deep depth of death, You heard my cries, Lord. You tossed me into this cold ocean and I sank into these dark frigid waters and the ocean waves cast themselves over me, then I cried out to You, Lord. "Your rejection has broken me... how will I ever lay eyes on Your holy temple again?"

Deeper I sank and death approached me as close as the water that surrounded me... seaweed grabbed my head and wrapped its twines around me. Downward I dropped to the mountain bottoms that rise up from the ocean floors. Yes, imprisoned / locked out / life was ebbing away as I sank deeper and deeper... but because of Your great mercy, You saved me, Lord, saved from the very jaws of death... all hope lost... yet

You heard my prayer even in the silence of that deep hole I found myself in / and yet those who worship gods they created ignore Your great mercies offered to all who would embrace them. Oh, Lord, know I will never worship anyone but You and You alone. How could I do less, Lord, seeing how You have saved me from such as I am in. I will, Lord, fulfill my promise to You for my deliverance is from You and You alone.

PURPOSE OF PRAYER

Jonah found himself in the belly of a whale so in a prayer of desperation, he tells the Lord he will be obedient from here on out.

JONAH 4:2-3

Oh, Lord, I knew You would decide to do what You have done in forgiving this nation of evilness. When I was in my own country and You told me to come over here... I did my utmost to flee to Tarshish because, Lord, I well know You are a God of mercy / very slow to anger / filled with kindness / so in knowing that, I was aware You have the ability to cancel a plan to destroy this people. Kill me, Lord, as I would rather be dead than alive for nothing I told these people is now going to happen.

PURPOSE OF PRAYER

Jonah was upset at God that He decided to not destroy the city of Nineveh because Jonah's preaching caused them to change their ways from evil to good.

HABAKKUK

HABAKKUK 1:2-4

Oh, Lord, how long... how much time will pass before You hear my cries? My words go to You as clouds disappear... and no answer. I cry out in vain, "Murderers, help," but no one comes to save. Lord, must I sit by and watch this sin and sadness that surrounds me as a fence. I look here and bribery is at it again. I look there and oppression raises its ugly head again, men fighting / arguing and loving it... is a disgrace to your nation / laws not enforced / justice unseen / courts as wicked as those who stand before judges. Yes, it can be said evil outweighs goodness in numbers unable to count.

PURPOSE OF PRAYER

The prophet was discouraged at the beginning of his ministry, yet his words are what God had instilled within him to say to those who would listen.

HABAKKUK 1:12-17

Oh, Lord my God, the holiest of holy, You, Lord, who has no beginning and no ending, I must ask my Lord, is it Your plan to end the Jewish race on planet earth? Surely this cannot be so. You, Lord, are our Rock and yet You have allowed by Your own will that these Chaldeans should rise above us to correct us in our sinful ways? Yes... agreed, Lord, we are a sinful people, but I ask... are they not more than us? Oh, Lord, will You who cannot stand sin in any form, allow them to swallow us up as a deer laps at their water to drink? Will You close Your eyes / plug up Your ears, Lord, while this evilness destroys those that are better than they?

Lord, are we but fish ready to be caught and butchered. Are we things of no value who have no leader to defend us from our archenemy? Must You allow them the right to put us on fish hooks and then drag around in their nets while they rejoice over their catch? If they are allowed to do that, Lord, they will in turn worship the nets that caught us and even burn incense before these self-made gods... and then to top it off... they will yell in bragging, "These gods shall make us rich." Oh Lord, how long will You allow such evil? Forever, Lord?

PURPOSE OF PRAYER

The prophet calls out to God to understand how greater evil can overcome lesser evil ... he pleads to understand God's judgment.

HABAKKUK 3:2-19

Oh, Lord, hallelujah for I have heard Your words and I, at minimum, can worship You, in awe of who You are. You are a God to be feared with the power and wisdom You have. You're going to work amongst us, and that, Lord, is a fearful thing in itself. Yes, Lord, again we are in deep need of You... and as You have done innumerable times in past eons, You alone have provided an escape... a way to save us... yet in Your anger against us, I plead, Lord, show as much love and mercy as You have shown in the history of this rebellious nation.

Oh, Lord, I must admit it is an amazing event, seeing You moving across the deserts from Mount Sinai. Your splendor, Lord, fills the earth and sky, and yes, the heavens as well... and because of You... all earth sings in praise of who You are. You are as wonderful as the prophets have said You are. From Your hand, light arrives / from Your voice, power is set in motion. Pestilence and plagues... all bow to Your command. When You stop Lord, and look at this creation of Yours... a word from Your mouth shakes the nations / making mountains fall / and hills to crumble. With You, Lord, nothing changes. All is as it's always been and all the future will be as it is this moment. Those in Cushan and Midian shake in the sandals they wear.

Oh, Lord, who can create something out of nothing but You. The seas parted creating land. Salvation for humankind created by You springs from nothing, created by You. The earth watched and waited for a word from Your mouth, and even the sea's deepest area whispered out loud, "We surrender." The sun and moon bowed as well, knowing it was You who created them. Yes, Lord, who but You has the power to march over nations, crushing them as You go. Yet, in all this anger, You never forgot the family You chose to call Your own. You put Satan on notice and crushed him and laid him out bare, head to toe.

And, as this nation of Israel, all thought for sure it would be an easy prey, but You stepped in and put a stop to their evilness. You sent angels on horseback riding on the ocean's top... And Lord, know when I see and hear all this, my lips tremble / my legs buckle / I literally shake in fear of Your awesomeness... yet now, Lord, still me / quiet me as I simply lay in wait for that day when You will crush those that would do harm to this nation You call Your own.

And know, please, my God, that even if all the fig trees are destroyed / that no blossom or fruit arrives / and even if all the olive crops fail to grow / and all the fields lie barren and unproductive, and yes, even if all the livestock died in their tracks, and the barns lay empty of anything worthwhile / I will continue to rejoice in You Lord. I will be happy in You, Lord, the God who saved me. You are my strength and will give me all I need to do Your will... be it the speed of a deer, and will as well, see to it my journey over the mountain is one of safety and security.

PURPOSE OF PRAYER

The prophet realizes God is all powerful / all encompassing / all wisdom / all fearful... so he prays a prayer of attempting to understand this God who has put within the prophet a wee bit of wisdom of who the creator is.

ZECHARIAH

ZECHARIAH 1:12-17

Oh, Lord of the earth and all it beholds. Now, seventy years have gone by and Your anger, Lord, still lays on Jerusalem and Judah. How much longer, Lord, before You offer them mercy? (With that said, God spoke to the angel next to me, passing on words to comfort and assurance... and with that, the angel's prayer continued, now answering the question.)

Do you not think I care for Judah and Jerusalem? You could compare me to a husband whose wife has been held captive. Yes, the heathen nations that are prosperous and found living easy think all is well even though they have put hardship on my own people. To that evilness I will now show mercy to Jerusalem. The temple will be rebuilt as all Israel will as well. Prosperity will overflow Israel as a day's water falls over its edge. The Lord of Earth will once again bless Jerusalem and will live within her.

PURPOSE OF PRAYER

An angel of God prayed this prayer knowing God had allowed punishment to Israel, but also found favor with his own and blessed them.

NEW
TESTAMENT
PRAYERS
TO
GOD

TABLE OF CONTENTS NEW TESTAMENT

MATTHEW

MATTHEW 6:9-13

Your Father knows what you need before you even whisper a prayer, yet here is a prayer you can pray that has merit behind it.

Our Father, who resides in Heaven, Know, Lord, we honor Your most holy Name, and we simply ask that Your kingdom arrive today, and Lord, may Your will always be done here on Your created Earth as it is in the Heavens You live in. We ask, Lord, to give us our need of food for today, and as always, Lord, forgive us our sins just as we work at forgiving others who have sinned against us. In addition, Lord, don't allow temptation to hound us, yet please, Lord, keep Satan from us so that we may work at doing Your will. Amen.

PURPOSE OF PRAYER

Folks asked Jesus how and what to pray... this was His response.

MATTHEW 26:39

Oh, Father of mine, if it would be possible, allow that which is about to be poured upon me to be removed. Yet know, Father, I am here to do Your will, not mine.

MATTHEW 20:42

On my Father, if this to be done to me is Your will, then let it be so.

PURPOSE OF PRAYERS

Jesus Christ knew what the future held for Him and it tore at Him so greatly that He prayed these two prayers.

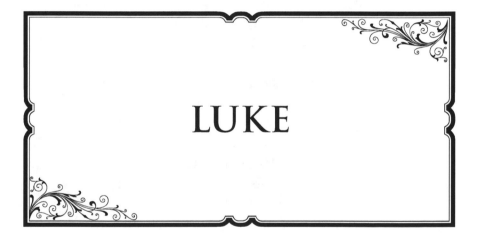

LUKE

LUKE 1:46-55

You believed by faith the angel's words. Oh, how I praise the God of Israel. How wonderful He is to me, my Savior. He peeked down from the heavens and saw a servant to Him, and because of His blessings, all future generations shall remember how I was chosen by God to be blessed by Him. He is the Lord. The Mighty One... has done miraculous things unto me. Yes, it can be tested by generations past that His mercy is beyond measure and will continue for the generations to follow and especially to those who abide by His word.

The awesomeness of Him alone is too great for simply mere words. He scatters those who think they are proud, and to those whose arrogance walks in front of them. He takes the high and mighty and replaces them with the low and nobody... to the hungry he feeds, and yet the rich leave empty handed.

Oh how He loves Israel. When the Lord makes a promise, one can be sure it will not be broken. He promised Abraham and his children, and to this day, we abound in those promises. Oh, Lord, be merciful to Israel forever.

PURPOSE OF PRAYER

The mother of Jesus finds she is thought to be worthy to bring the Christ child into the world and this is her reaction to such heavenly actions.

LUKE 2:29-32

Oh, my God, My Lord, You have kept Your promise and now I can be a contented man. I have witnessed with my own eyes the Savior You have given to the world. He is the light that will shine in darkness. All nations will know who He is and He will be Your representative for Israel.

PURPOSE OF PRAYER

Simeon was in the temple of God when Mary and Joseph came to dedicate their son, Jesus Christ, to the Lord, and he had been told via the Spirit of God that he would not die before he had actually seen the Messiah.

LUKE 23:24

Father, forgive these people. They have no idea what they are doing!

PURPOSE OF PRAYER

Jesus Christ had been falsely accused, falsely found guilty, falsely tortured, falsely put to death on a cruel cross, yet He knew why He was born, which was His situation at the moment.

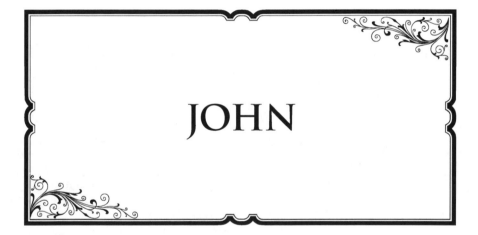

JOHN

JOHN 11:41-43

Father, thank You... thank You... for hearing my request. And yes, I am well aware You always hear me, but my words were spoken aloud so that those standing in this crowd will come to believe it was You who sent me, Father.

"Lazarus – come out!"

PURPOSE OF PRAYER

Jesus prayed this prayer upon raising Lazarus from the dead.

JOHN 17:1-26

Oh, Father, the time You have chosen for me has come. Now, Father, reveal the glory in Me, Your Son, so that I may give the glory back to You. You, Father, and You alone, have given this Son of Yours all authority over every human being on this planet Earth You alone created. And Father, all those souls You give to me, I in turn give them eternal life for the only way to this life of eternal living is to know You, Father, the only true God who is in control of all that there is and to have a faith in me, Jesus Christ, the One You sent to earth. All You said to do has been done and the glory of that belongs to You. Oh Father, let my glory shine as I stand here in Your presence... this marvelous glory we together shared before the foundation of this Earth was formed.

Oh, Father, I have shared here with these individuals who You are. They belong to the world, but You chose them to be part of me, Father, and I am deeply grateful for their lives and they, Father, have been obedient to You... and You have opened their minds, Father, so that they now know all I am and all I have is a gift directly from You. They have heard their commands I have spoken and they know these as well came from You, Father. They believe for they have seen and are a witness to Your awesome power, Father.

I do not plead for this world, but I do plead for these You have given to me to care over, and yet, since they are mine because of You, they are also Yours, Father. These then are my glory. And yet soon, I am leaving them to come home where I left to come here. So, again, I plead with You to watch over them... protect them and unite them as You and I are united. While here, Father, I have kept safe and have kept them safe as well as have guarded their souls so that none were lost to the son of evil (only one, Father, left the fold and now he sits in his due place as the scriptures foretold by the prophets of old).

Yes, Father, I am on my way home and many a time I have told this to those You gave me so that they would be in joy for my return. I have fulfilled Your commands and yes, this world hates me for all I have done and said because none of it fits in with their belief system. So I plead, again, keep these You have entrusted to me safe from the horrendous power of Satan. They, Father, do not belong to this world just as I don't, so make them pure and holy by teaching them those things You put into me. You sent me here... I am coming home... so I am sending them out as You did me. Yes, Father, I commit to the truth, that I will be with them meeting their needs in truth and holiness.

PURPOSE OF PRAYER

Jesus Christ was sent by God to be introduced to the world... God Himself in human form. He lived thirty-three years. He came into the world miraculously and He left in the same miraculous way. This is His prayer for those He entrusted the future of His words and acts of miracles.

ACTS

ACTS 1:25

Oh, Lord, we plead with You, look down upon this fragile group of men, and as You know as an open book, we ask You to point to the man of Your choice to replace Judas who betrayed the Messiah... the One from You... Jesus Christ. A traitor from birth Judas was, but now is the time to move on with the work You have for us to do so You point him out, Lord.

PURPOSE OF PRAYER

The men chosen by Jesus had gotten together to choose the individual to take Judas Iscariot's place. Matthias was chosen.

ACTS 4:24-30

Oh, Lord of all creation, be it earth, sun, moon, stars, the heavens above and the sea below. Eons ago, You put into King David, by the Holy Spirit, a message for us today and the generations to come. "The unfaithful / non-believers / heathen rage / spit / yell / curse God as if He was blind and deaf, yet He sees it all and hears it all... foolish as they are plotting against God as if He were some mortal being and yet they battle against Him as they do against the One He sent to save them." Such fools they are.

PURPOSE OF PRAYER

The Jewish council just had Peter and John arrested for preaching about Jesus Christ. But after Peter gave them a sermon they would not soon forget, they released them and Peter and John went back to the others and all united in this prayer.

ACTS 7:59-60

Oh, Lord, please receive my spirit... and as well, Lord, don't blame these who have committed this sinful error.

PURPOSE OF PRAYER

Stephen had just given a miraculous sermon about the Messiah, Jesus Christ, but when he stated that the crowd in front of him was responsible for the crucifixion of the Messiah, the Jewish leaders became enraged with guilt and shame... so to stomp out this inner feeling they took him to the outskirts of town and stoned him to death. These are the last words Stephen spoke before his soul went home.

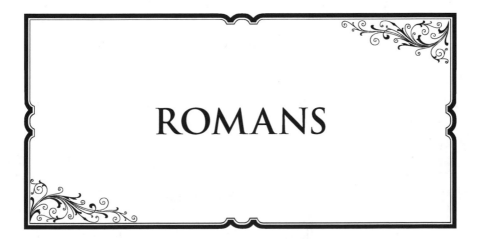

ROMANS

ROMANS 15:30-32

I ask you, will you stand by me in prayer? Will you become partners? Will you do this for the one we preach about, Jesus Christ, and as well... for the love you have shown me which was put within you by the Holy Spirit Himself? I ask you...

1) Pray my work continues with much success for God.
2) Pray for my protection from non-Christians while I am in Jerusalem.
3) Pray the Christians in Jerusalem will be acceptable to the monies we bring them.

If God answers the above, then I can come with a happy heart and a contented soul... and this way we can refresh each of us.

May the God of our being give you the peace you seek. Amen.

PURPOSE OF PRAYER

Paul is telling his followers how his life is to be a messenger of God from above, and now he is about to enter a city, which has been difficult on the Christians living there... so he pleads for their prayers.

2ND CORINTHIANS

2ND CORINTHIANS 13:7-9

My prayer is you live out your journey working at being good, decent, honest... and above all... godly. And don't live this way for the sake of being thanked for it.... no, do it because it's your Christian responsibility. And by all means... even if those who hate us... reject our message... our work is to do this – "Keep living right / teaching what's right / and turning our backs on evilness." If we have to lose for you to win... so be it. Our greatest, most important goal, is to see you grow from children to adults in your Christian journey.

PURPOSE OF PRAYER

This is the third visit of Paul to the church of Corinth. He is, as always, appealing to them to run after what is godly and run away from evil.

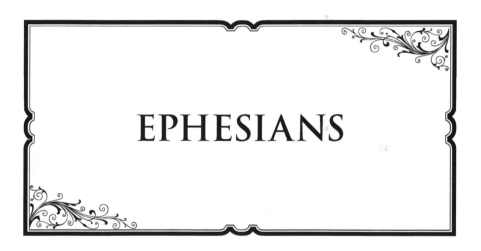

EPHESIANS

EPHESIANS 1:15-23

I have heard of your faith in Jesus Christ and I thank God for you and this strong faith you have... and the love you have shown for other Christians is from the source of love, God Himself. Know please, that it's you I thank God for, and it's you I ask God to pour wisdom into so that you truly grasp whom this Jesus Christ really is and what He's doing for you on a day-in and day-out basis. Please know my prayer is for you to be flooded with light so that your future is not clouded with darkness.

Know this as well, God is surely richer today for the souls that are His which are in you. This power that has saved you, as well raised Jesus Christ from the dead, now has been placed in you and to all that believe by faith. Yes, it can be said in truth that Jesus Christ sits at God's right hand and has been given powers far greater than mere dictators or rulers for His is above all else... be it today or all the future to arrive. He, this Jesus Christ, is the head of His church. He is the first and last / the author and giver of all that sustains everything anywhere.

PURPOSE OF PRAYER

Paul writes this to the church of Ephesus because he is doing his utmost to describe to them what they have within their possession... Freedom from death with God / an escape from Hell / a way out of Satan's grip. This is his prayer for them.

EPHESIANS 3:14-21

When I consider the overall plan of God, I am in awe and it literally buckles my knees in praise for His wondrous wisdom. Yes, many of those in this plan now wait in heaven for our homecoming and yet while here we have this glorious gift from the Holy Spirit. Oh, my prayer is sincere that Jesus Christ will flood your hearts in living out a life of faith in Him. May your souls have roots deep enough that God's love pours out of your lives and in that root may you get a glimpse of the depth / the width / the height of His love for this creation of His.

Yet, never be discouraged in knowing how long you live / what your journey encompasses. Will you ever comprehend remotely the full understanding of this love God has, and especially for those that return His love. Yes, it can safely be said there is a power within you that will allow you to do far greater things than you ever dreamed... far above the imagination... even above our loftiest prayers / hopes / thoughts / motivations.

May God always be given the glory He so richly deserves for eternity. Know this, the God I speak of has put together a plan of salvation that is so full of wisdom that the foolish are blind to it.

PURPOSE OF PRAYER

Paul lays out God's plan of mankind's escape from hell in this prayer to the church at Ephesus.

EPHESIANS 6:18-20

Always pray... always ask God for what you need. Make sure those needs line up with the Holy Spirit's wishes for you. Yes, plead with God... cry out to Him... constantly remind Him you need Him, and do not forget to pray for Christians worldwide.

PURPOSE OF PRAYER

Paul's last part of this letter to the church of Ephesus, he warns them of the war Satan will have upon Christians and that prayer is the greatest weapon Christianity has to defend itself.

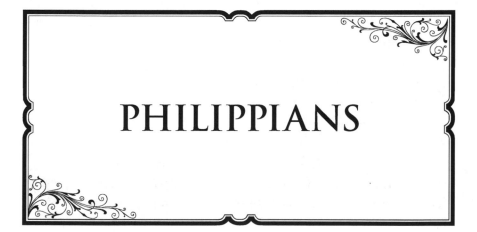

PHILIPPIANS

PHILIPPIANS 1:1-11

This is from your brothers in Jesus Christ / Paul and Timothy / to all you pastors and deacons and the Christians of the church of Philippi.

My prayer is for you to each receive all the blessings God so richly passes out to those who love Him and may this blessing bring peace in your hearts and on your journey through life.

My prayer is for you ... come from God filled with joy knowing how you are distributing this awesome message of Jesus Christ. This work you are putting forth will as well, help you grow in your own Christian walk until that wonderful day when He, the Messiah, makes His return here to Earth.

I am sure you are aware of my deep feelings for you as you have a special place within my heart for it was through you I shared my joy while imprisoned and while free of prison. Yet, only God truly knows my love for you... so my continued prayer for you is this: "That you will so overflow with love for your fellow brothers and sisters, and all humanity that those without Christ will want what you have... and by this, your growth in the Lord will sprout as a young plant bursting out of the ground it was planted in."

Stay planted in knowing right vs. wrong / stay clean / don't allow anyone to have a reason to criticize you / do good / be kind / all this will prove you are born from above and will bring glory to God.

PURPOSE OF PRAYER

Paul loved, as he did all, this church in Philippi and he prayed earnestly for their journey with God as their leader.

PHILIPPIANS 1:19

You can be sure gladness fills my heart knowing you are praying for me for the Holy Spirit is doing its own work in continuing to assure me all is going to turn out for my own good.

PURPOSE OF PRAYER

Paul knows death is on the horizon... so here he assures the church of Philippi that regardless of his outcome, both will glorify God.

PHILIPPIANS 4:6-7

Do not, and I emphasize, do not worry about anything... yet you should pray about everything. Yes, let God know your needs, and as well, thank Him when they arrive. By having this simple life-changing attitude, you will have that inner peace that the human mind cannot possibly comprehend as it is foreign to His thoughts. Trust in Jesus Christ and that alone will quiet the restless soul.

PURPOSE OF PRAYER

Paul tells the church members the secret of peace within.... knowing full well it works as it has for him, yet how many will learn its ways.

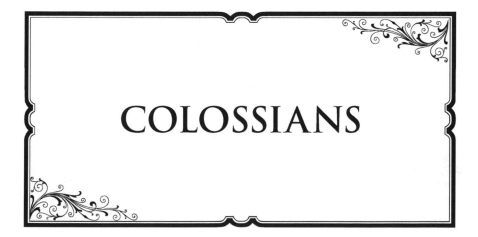

COLOSSIANS

COLOSSIANS 1:3

Our first thoughts of you are in praying for you and in giving thanks to God for your faith in Jesus Christ.

PURPOSE OF PRAYER

Paul always loved and respected the churches he had developed, and in some way, it all began through the power of his Savior.

COLOSSIANS 1:11

You can be assured we are in deep prayer that you be filled up with the power and the strength of God so that you cannot be stopped by the forces that would stop you, if allowed. Stay joyful in God.

PURPOSE OF PRAYER

Paul, here, is again assuring the church in Colosse that God is in the work they are doing on His behalf.

COLOSSIANS 4:2-6

Never get tired of praying. Keep at it 24 / 7 / 365, and watch how God answers... and be thankful when they arrive. Pray for us so that we will have many, many chances to preach this great news of Jesus Christ... which is why, at this moment, I sit here shackled in a jail. Yes, pray for me whether I am jailed or free, God will put within me the boldness to make the message so simple a child could comprehend it... and you as well, take every opportunity to do likewise. Use wisdom with those you mingle with and let your words always be gracious and understandable... as then, folks will be able to take in what you have to say.

PURPOSE OF PRAYER

Paul warns those who speak out to use wisdom with those they share the gospel, and yet be bold in their presentation.

1ST THESSALONIANS

1ˢᵀ THESSALONIANS 1:2-3

Always... always... always... we thank God for you and pray for you constantly. Your deeds are etched in us as our blood runs through our veins. We even speak to God about you... and how strong your faith has blossomed... and how eagerly you look to the day Jesus Christ returns.

PURPOSE OF PRAYER

Paul is assuring those at the church of Thessalonica that he has not forgotten them, but instead thinks of them daily.

1ˢᵀ THESSALONIANS 3:11-13

May we return to you soon... is our hope and prayer, and may God Himself make a way for that to happen. Please, I request of you, in my absence, to love one another, and all those you come into contact with... as you have seen me reach out with love to you. By doing this, your hearts will grow strong / sinless / holy... for by doing this, you will one day stand before God guiltless when Jesus Christ returns the victor.

PURPOSE OF PRAYER

Paul tells the church to stand firm in its faith in the One who saves their souls from the one who would steal it if he could.

2ND THESSALONIANS

2ND THESSALONIANS 1:11-12

Our prayers never cease in asking God to mold you into that which is pleasing to Him. Yes, to make you as you think you could be and rewarding you for such lives you will live out... by all seeing this in You... they will shout praises to God for this newfound life they see in you belonging to Jesus Christ can be your most ambitious goal in life... so strive towards that, and know it's that tender love of God that has created all you're seeing in the changes you have made.

PURPOSE OF PRAYER

This is Paul's second letter to this church and again he emphasizes the necessity to hold tight to God in all aspects of their daily living.

2ⁿᵈ THESSALONIANS 3:1-5

Just as my letter began it as well has an ending so, I again ask, "Pray for us" and as well pray:

The message of Jesus Christ spreads like wildfire and that it wins souls daily.

That we will be saved from the evilness created by Satan... and from the hands of evil men, for not all love God as one would think.

Know this, God is faithful and will make you strong enough to win the war over your souls. So we are trusting in God that you daily, put into practice all that we taught you. May God so work within you that you will come to a deep understanding of the love of God and His patience with you.

PURPOSE OF PRAYER

Paul sternly tells the church to watch for those who would do harm to the gospel they preach knowing full well the intentions of Satan are for one thing only – evil.

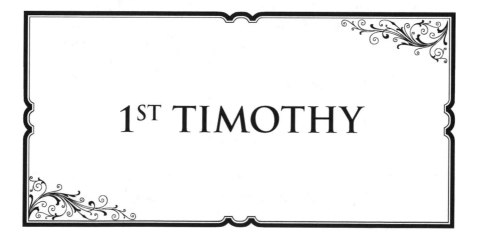

1ST TIMOTHY

1ST TIMOTHY 2:1-6

Take my advice, always pray for others. Plead that God has mercy on their souls and give thanks for all He does for them and you.

Pray for all those who have authority over us... be it a king or the law of the land... for by doing this, you will find you can live with contentment and peace and a quiet spirit. Yes, I urge you to spend your time living out Godly lives and giving much thought to God in all His ways. This, I can assure you pleases God and know that God longs for all humanity to be saved, but as well know this truth, "God is on one side and humanity is on the other, and it's only Jesus Christ that has the awesome ability to build a bridge between the two sides. He gave us His life for one and only purpose."

PURPOSE OF PRAYER

In this letter, Paul tells Timothy that even though mankind has no way to interact with God because of sin... Jesus Christ came to bridge that gap.

2ND TIMOTHY

2ND TIMOTHY 1:3

Oh, Timothy, please know I pray for you in earnest daily, and how I thank God for who you are. Yes, 24 / 7 / 365, I pray for you, be it morning or the wee hours of a morning. I plead... beg God to bless you so richly you will shout for joy knowing He has answered my humble request... for my only purpose in being is to serve and please Him... nothing else matters.

PURPOSE OF PRAYER

Paul loves this disciple he has worked and trained, and he tells him here those very words.

PHILEMON

PHILEMON 1:4-7

Know Philemon that I always thank God for who you are. The messages I hear from others of your love for God and trust in Him inspires me to no end. Yes, I pray your message of God will grip others as it has you, and that others will see in you a life they want a part of. I, as many others, have benefited from the love you demonstrate in your walk with God. Thank you for being a brother in Jesus Christ and for your freshness of what Christianity is all about.

PURPOSE OF PRAYER

Paul writes to this disciple as he did Timothy... one to build up in confidence that the life he has chosen was the right one... for the right time... and for the right reasons.

HEBREWS

HEBREWS 13:18-19

Please pray for us... especially that our conscience is clear, and plead for it to stay that way... and as well, pray for me that God may make a way for me to return to you sooner rather than later.

PURPOSE OF PRAYER

The writer has written a long letter detailing much of how Christianity came about, and the wisdom God showed with a plan. Now he asks God to return him home to where he belongs.

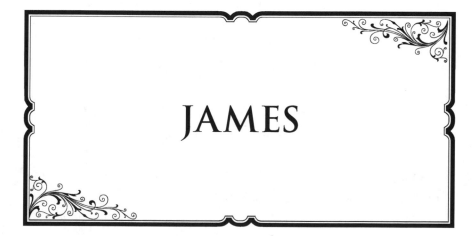

JAMES

JAMES 5:14-18

Are you sick? Is anyone sick? If so, then by all means call in the elders of the church and they in unison should pray over the sick. Pour some holy oil on them... for it is God who has the power to heal, and prayer with faith will find the conclusion to be a healthy body... and if the sickness was caused by sin, the Lord has the power to forgive such.

So I urge you, admit your errors / mistakes / faults / misjudgments to one another and that alone will heal the wounds caused by such. Prayer has power and awesome results. Take Elijah... as normal as you and I, yet when he prayed no rain would fall. It didn't for three and a half years. Then he prayed again and it poured making all the dryness turn to greenery.

PURPOSE OF PRAYER

James, the brother of Jesus Christ, tells the Jewish Christians how to be healed and how to live out a Godly life.

1ˢᵀ PETER

1ˢᵀ PETER 3:8-12

Listen to my sound advice, please. Work at being one large family, filled with happiness for one another, and as well, with empathy for one another, and naturally loving one another as you love your own selves. Be tender with one another. Be humble in your view of your own selves. Don't sit around thinking how you can get back at another who has wronged you in some way. Don't repay anger with anger. My advice is to pray for God to always help in the good and bad situations. Yes, be kind and work at it as you would work at whatever it is you do for a living... and by doing this, rest assured God will bless you for such living out your journey.

If you truly seek a life that can be rewarding, here are some Godly tips:

1) Keep control of your tongue
2) Stay away from lying
3) Run from evil...yet run after goodness
4) Run after peace as if it were a race to win God's approval

God's eyes view the entire world. Nothing escapes Him no matter how dark or deep the situation. And know this, God's ears hear every prayer... be it from a child whimpering a prayer, or the elderly whispering a prayer. Yet know this, God is not easy on those who live and produce evil.

PURPOSE OF PRAYER

Peter was an apostle of the Lord Jesus Christ. Here he gives sound advice as to how to live out the Christian journey with prayer as a major component of that journey.

1ST PETER 4:7

Soon this world as we know it will come to its final chapter. So knowing that, I solemnly urge you to be men of prayer, dedicating your lives to this important part of the Christian journey.

PURPOSE OF PRAYER

Peter knew the importance of prayer and he greatly emphasized that all men of God stay at such... a great communication between them and God.

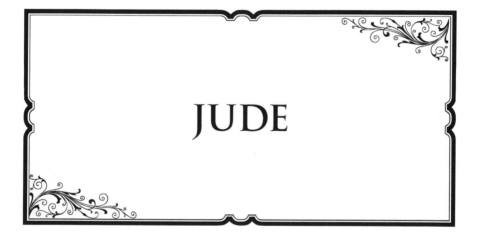

JUDE

JUDE 1:20

Dear friends, build your lives on this one foundation – "Faith in Jesus Christ" and pray through the glorious power of the Holy Spirit working on your behalf.

PURPOSE OF PRAYER

Jude was a brother of the Messiah, Jesus Christ. He wrote a one-chapter letter, yet in it, he advised the one communicator between the believer and God – "prayer."

Printed in the United States
By Bookmasters